ORION PLAIN AND SIMPLE

body
reading

SASHA FENTON

Previously published in 2009 as *Body Reading* by
Zambezi Publishing Limited, Devon, UK

This edition first published in Great Britain in 2017 by
Orion
an imprint of the Orion Publishing Group Ltd
Carmelite House, 50 Victoria Embankment,
London, EC4Y 0DZ
An Hachette UK Company

1 3 5 7 9 10 8 6 4 2

Interior design by Kathryn Sky-Peck

A CIP catalogue record for this book is available
from the British Library.

Paperback ISBN: 978 1 4091 6957 4

eBook ISBN: 978 1 4091 6958 1

Printed and bound by CPI Group (UK), Ltd, Croydon, CR0 4YY

www.orionbooks.co.uk

Contents

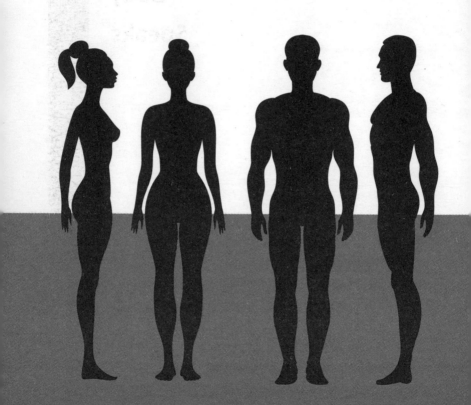

The
Body
Speaks

N
T
R
O
D
U
C
T
I
O
N

In the 1980s, I wrote several books for the late, much lamented Aquarian Press. One day while at their offices, the then editor, David Brawn, suggested that I write a book on what you can read from a person's body. He went on to say that he didn't want a book on body language, but on what you can tell about a person from various parts of the body, in the same way that a palmist can deduce the character and destiny of a person from their hands.

After a bit of thought, I decided that it could be done, although the research would take time. As it happened, it took several months and it involved quite a bit of traveling. I spoke to many people about a variety of divinations and health methods, and I even took my dentist out for a drink! Some people were very helpful. I particularly remember Hazel, a really wonderful reflexologist, who gave me a reflexology treatment while describing her work. As it happened, some weeks before going to see Hazel, I had cracked a bone in my wrist, and Hazel picked up the weakness, despite the fact that there was no bandage or cast on my arm to show that anything was wrong. I was most impressed!

Nowadays, people take their information from the Internet. There's a lot of data to be found, but it isn't always exactly what you need when researching complex, non-mainstream issues, so there is still no substitute for talking to real, live people on the phone or in person—people who actually study various parts of the body. But at that time, in the 1980s, it also meant digging out my collection of Victorian fortune-telling books and scouring second hand shops for more of them. It turned out to be great fun and well worth the effort.

The other thing that required an effort on my part was the illustrations, as all I had to fall back on was my own talent and ability (or lack of it) so the illustrations and cartoons are also all my own work. I've now resurrected the original book, stripped out the waffle and updated it, as new discoveries happen every day.

You may disagree with the Victorians' observations, or mine; that's perfectly acceptable. Ultimately, what counts is reality, nothing is written in stone and there are always exceptions to every rule. What this book does convey are conclusions drawn from many actual case studies, and you should form your own opinion, in conjunction with this book and any sources of a similar nature.

As you delve more into the art of body reading, your own research and observations will become part of your analytical repertoire.

I hope you enjoy dipping into this book as much as I enjoyed writing it.

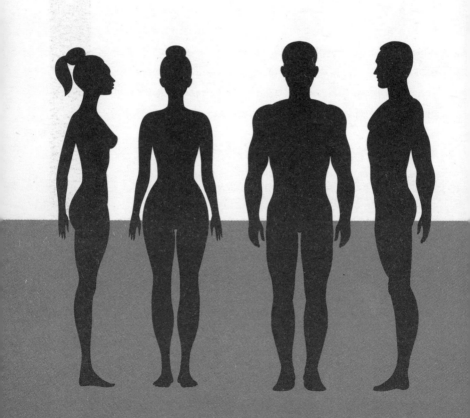

Hair

1

There are people who specialize in radiasthesia, whereby the practitioner holds a pendulum over a lock of hair in order to ascertain his client's state of health. He then usually goes on to suggest specific types of food and drugs to correct problems.

Radiasthesia is well known and well documented, but character divination by hair is not. In fact, apart from my own observation of people, added to a few old wives' tales, I wasn't aware that anything of the kind existed. Well, I was wrong. The Victorians, those indefatigable observers of human appearance and behavior, had already come to their own conclusions; but more of that in the following pages.

Our hair reflects our state of health and our state of mind. It normally grows roughly at the rate of half an inch per month, but this growth slows down when a person is overtired or ill. Some of us "moult" in the spring, and everybody finds that there are times when we seem to lose some of our hair and other times when it grows abundantly. It's common knowledge that women experience some hair loss after having a baby, or when they stop taking any type of hormone therapy, including contraceptive pills. Obviously, there are some specific medical conditions, such as alopecia, that affect the hair, but generally speaking, if a subject is fit and happy, his or her hair will shine.

It's widely perceived that red-haired people are hot tempered and that bald men are sexy, but I've noticed over the years that there are other characteristics. For example, a faded blonde with weak and flimsy hair may be unable to take control of her life. She may be dominated by her husband and taken for granted by her children. Very strong straight hair, the kind that has a will of its own, belongs to an independent, strong-minded person who isn't likely to compromise on anything. This type of person is proud and self-centred, although not altogether selfish or thoughtless. Such people may delay taking on commitments until they are sure that they can cope with them. Another utterly uncompromising type is the person who has tight African-type curls. This person is unusual to the point of eccentricity. I have three acquaintances who have this kind of hair. One loves horses, another is an actor, and the third writes historical novels. Those who have baby-fine, flimsy hair have great ideas, but they lack the energy or confidence to bring their ideas to life. Also, those with fine hair tend to be sensitive. Those with coarser hair are less sensitive and less interested in the feelings of others.

The rest of us muddle along, sticking with the same hairstyle for years, unless we become ill, busy, or despondent, when we may suddenly cut the lot off.

And then of course is the whole issue of coloring hair, and permanently changing the texture through perms and straighteners. This has become more and more common in our modern times. When interpreting a person's hair, start with their natural hair—color and type—and then add the additional interpretation of what the person willfully changed his or her hair to.

Some Ideas from the Victorians

Color and texture

A woman with medium strong straight hair enjoys socializing, but she is reliable in relationships. Her health is neither especially vigorous nor especially weak. She is moderate, thoughtful and not likely to go overboard in matters of love.

A man with thick, very smooth, very black hair worn long is mild but firm, cool unless provoked, and normally moderate in his behavior. He is reliable in relationships and generally lucky in love.

A man with short, black, curly hair tends to be drunken, quarrelsome, oversexed, unstable, and unreliable in his undertakings. He will be enthusiastic at the beginning of an enterprise, but will lose heart as time goes on. He wants to be rich, but he will be disappointed in this ambition.

The same can be said for a woman with this type of hair, but she will be steadier in relationships.

A man who has long, smooth, brown hair will be healthy, obstinate, enthusiastic, fond of variety, curious and flexible in outlook. He will enjoy the company of women.

Men and women with short, bushy brown hair are also healthy, enthusiastic, fond of variety, curious and flexible in outlook and they both enjoy the company of the opposite sex, but both have hotter tempers.

A man with light brown, long, smooth hair is peaceful, generous and sensible. He will try to keep the peace between others, although when provoked, he could over-react and then be sorry afterward. He is fond of the ladies, but protective toward them. Overall, this man is friendly, cheerful and kind.

A woman with light brown, long, smooth hair is softhearted, but quick to anger. She is reasonable in relationships and her health is good. She will not be outstandingly lucky in life, and will have to work hard in order to achieve her goals.

A man with fair hair may have poor health and may be too inward looking. He could be too interested in religious matters. He will work hard, keep himself to himself and be disinclined to run after women, but in spite of all this piety, he will have a difficult life.

A woman with fair hair is healthy, purposeful, passionate, but difficult in a relationship. She loves to be praised for her beauty, she enjoys exercise and she will live a long life.

A man with long, red hair enjoys business meetings and travel and is a great womanizer. He is always looking for ways to obtain money, but spends it like water when he has it. He is obstinate and determined and he will not give up when he has some objective that he wants in his sights. He is inwardly shy and nervous, but covers this up with bluster and gives an appearance of courage. He may be cunning and deceitful.

A woman with long, red hair is talkative and vain. Her temper is impatient and fiery and she is highly sexed. She may appear frail, but is surprisingly fit and strong, although she may not live to a ripe old age. She is impulsive and enthusiastic, but her attention wanders and she seldom sees things through. She becomes bitter and resentful when disappointed.

Hair placement

Hair that falls forward over the forehead indicates a rational person who is easily duped. According to Victorian books, this person will frequently be short of money.

Hair falling forward over the forehead

Hair that lies backward denotes a person who is obstinate, peevish and passionate. People with this kind of hair are bossy and quick to anger if they are not immediately obeyed by others. They are entertaining storytellers, they are good with their families and they are good providers.

Hair that lies backward

Hair that grows low on the forehead indicates a person who is selfish and designing, unsociable, a drinker and has a greedy and scheming nature. The Victorians really had it in for this characteristic!

Hair that grows low on the forehead

And finally, hair that is balding. What can I say? —bald men are sexy!

A Few Hairy Facts

Some groups lay down rules about hair, and this is especially the case with religious people, most of whom—whatever religion they belong to—consider a woman's hair to be some kind of sexual come on, and thus something that should be partially or wholly covered. Others wear a certain style to identify them as being of a particular age or social group. For instance, young men and women will create a style and after a while, if their parents also take up the style, the youngsters go in for a totally different look to differentiate themselves once again.

- Sikh men don't cut their hair at all.

- Traditional types of Indian women don't cut their hair much, if at all.

- Orthodox Jewish men grow the hair at the sides of their heads into ringlets called "pyers."

- Orthodox Jewish women cut their hair short and wear wigs.

- Orthodox Muslim women cover their hair with a hijab.

- In the English Civil War, Cromwell's soldiers cut their hair to distinguish them from the Cavaliers.

- From the 19th century onward, soldiers started to wear their hair short to stay free of lice.

- Skinheads cut their hair to look "hard."

- In World War II, the Nazis shaved the heads of concentration camp inmates to remove their individuality.

- In France and elsewhere, after World War II, women who had collaborated with the Germans had their heads shaved in public.

- Rastafarians started the dreadlock style.

Until World War I, women always had long hair, which they put up as a mark of passing from childhood to becoming a young adult. During the war, they started to shorten their hair, due to working in factories and in transport, where long hair was a nuisance at best and dangerous at worst.

After World War I, women's lives and their roles changed radically from the Edwardian world that had preceded the war, so they marked this by cutting their hair and going in for the short, straight "bob" style.

If, when combing your hair, lots of it comes away, the odds are strong that you will come down with a serious illness. This belief very likely does have a basis in fact, because a number of illnesses do cause hair loss, probably in a kind of energy-saving campaign.

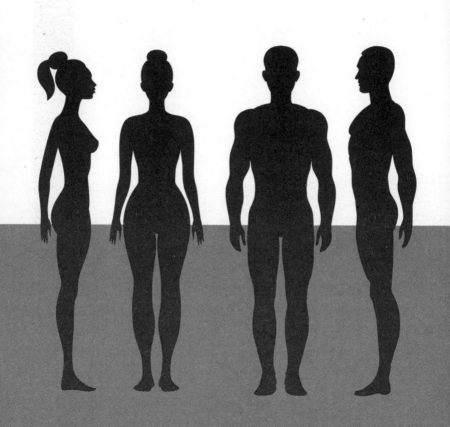

Heads

2

Our knowledge of the human mind and body, and much that we now take for granted in medicine and psychoanalysis is surprisingly new, but there are lines of research that were carried out in the 19th century that didn't stand the test of time in a practical sense. One such interest was phrenology, or assessing character by the bumps on a person's head.

Phrenology was originally developed by Dr. Gall, a native of Baden, who postulated that there is a connection between the ways in which the mind works and the shape of the cranium. His idea was that the shape of the head indicated the kind of brain contained within. He also suggested that a young person's brain could be altered by education and specific kinds of use. This latter statement has proved to be true, and not only for young people— elderly people are told by their doctors that if they want to keep their minds nimble, they must use them or lose them.

The first thing that the Victorian phrenologists did was to measure the size of the cranium, as that supposedly revealed the amount of brainpower within. It's normal for a woman's head to measure 48cm to 56cm, and for a man's head to measure 49cm to 57cm. There are, however, many exceptions to this rule.

The Seven Major Divisions

Having measured the head, they divided it into seven imaginary sections.

A Associated with the planet Mercury, this is considered the seat of the main intellect and the ability to think.

B Associated with the planet Jupiter, this concerns the things to which we find ourselves naturally drawn. It rules anything that captures our loyalty or devotion.

C Associated with the planet Saturn, this is concerned with our survival instincts. It rules our urge to protect and safeguard others and ourselves.

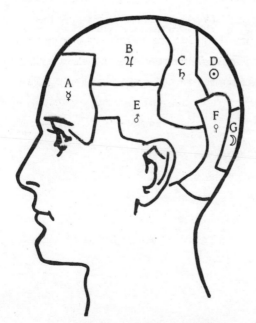

The seven major divisions of the head

D Associated with the Sun, this governs the whole workings of the mind. It's concerned with our ambitions and the way we set about achieving them.

E Associated with the planet Mars, this is concerned with our energies, natural instincts and appetites. It rules such things as our willingness to fight for what we want and the acquisition of material possessions.

F Associated with the planet Venus, this concerns matters of feeling and affection. It rules love and sex.

G Associated with the Moon, this concerns our relationship with our family, our home situation and our place in society.

The Forty-Two Areas of the Head

The Victorians divided the seven sections into a total of 42 sub-sections, and these can be seen in the following diagram.

Area A

1. Individuality

This involves the power of observation and the ability to discriminate. The larger the bump, the more the person likes dealing with details. If too large, he will be ultra-critical and very inquisitive. If too small, he will have little curiosity and very poor mental faculties.

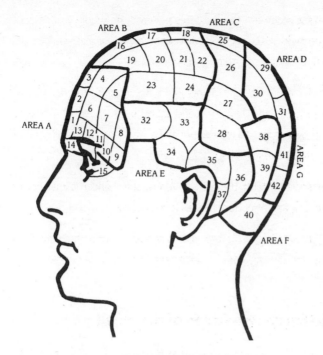

The 42 areas on the head

2. Eventuality

We know this as memory. A large bump implies a good memory, while a small one suggests a poor memory and a low level of intellect.

3. Comparison

This rules reasoning ability and powers of analysis. If over large, the subject may be hypercritical, if too small, the subject cannot make comparisons or apply himself.

4. Causality

The Victorians also called this "powers of deduction." If large, the subject has an original mind, good powers of deduction and intuition and he would make a good explorer or inventor; if small, the mind will be mundane and shallow.

5. Mirthfulness

This denotes a sense of humor. A small bump suggests that the subject can't see a joke.

6. Locality

This relates to a sense of direction and a memory for places. If large, the subject would have a photographic memory and he might even experience déjà vu at times! A small bump suggests that the subject finds visualization difficult and that he lacks a sense of direction.

7. Time

This links with a sense of rhythm and timing, as well as punctuality. A small bump suggests that the subject is never on time for anything and that he has no ear for rhythm.

8. Tune

If this bump is developed, the subject will have an ear for music. If not, he won't be able to sing in tune and may not appreciate music at all.

9. Calculation

A large bump here indicates an aptitude for figures, while a small one suggests poor numeric skills.

10. Order

If this bump is large, the subject will be well organized and able to work systematically. If it's small, he will be disorganized and confused.

11. Color

The person can judge shades of color and remember them; he can also distinguish distant objects. If large, the subject may be able to use color exceptionally creatively. If it's small, he will have difficulty in seeing objects at a distance and he may be color-blind.

12. Weight

This governs the ability to judge the weight of objects, along with the ability to balance objects on top of each other or to keep one's own balance. (People with large feet are better at keeping their balance than those with small feet, because it's easier to keep the body upright when the feet are large.)

13. Size

This governs the ability to judge the size of an object or space of a room.

14. Form

This concerns the ability to see and remember people and objects. Artistic people have a well developed bump here. An over-large bump may make for super-sensitivity to atmospheres and places, while a small one would indicate a subject who is oblivious to people and to his surroundings.

15. Language

A well-developed bump belongs to a good communicator who has a way with words. It also implies an ability to learn foreign languages. If over-large, the subject will talk too much. If small, he may be reticent or hesitant and fumbling in speech.

Area B

16. Humanity

Sometimes called the bump of intuition, this gives really deep understanding of the motivation of others. If underdeveloped, the subject cannot understand others and is indifferent to them.

17. Benevolence

If over-developed, the subject will be over-generous and too ready to help others. If under-developed, he is miserly with both his time and his money.

18. Veneration

This indicates a respect for values and traditions. If over-developed, the subject may be fanatical about religion. If the bump is small, he could hold nothing sacred and have a destructive nature.

19. Agreeableness

This symbolizes popularity, charm, and pleasantness. If overlarge, the subject could be effusive. If small, he is hostile and offensive.

20. Imitativeness

This is the ability to learn by imitation. A small bump here suggests independence and eccentricity or an inability to learn by imitation.

21. Spirituality

This relates to religious or spiritual feelings. If over-large, the subject might be too otherworldly to cope with daily life. If very small, the mind will only be able to cope with practical matters.

22. Hopefulness

This concerns optimism and forward thinking. Too large a bump here suggests a lack of realism, while too small a bump suggests a pessimist.

23. Ideality

This symbolizes an appreciation of beauty and nice things. If the bump is over-large, the subject will be unrealistic. If small, he lacks imagination, culture or ideals.

24. Sublimity

A love of romance, as in romantic scenery, thrilling experiences, the wild grandeur of places and appreciation of all that is best in life. If over-large, the subject may want to dramatize everything. If small, he will have absolutely no romance in his soul and will be a wet blanket.

Area C

25. Firmness

In moderation, this bump endows the subject with determination and self-discipline, but if it's over-large, he is a tyrant or a despot. If small, he will be irresponsible and unable to finish anything that he starts. He may be easily led into temptations or easily bullied by stronger people.

26. Conscientiousness

If this is over-developed, the subject will be nervous and neurotic. If small, he will be indifferent to the needs of others and he will lack principles.

27. Caution

If this bump is over-large, the subject will be too fearful to achieve anything. If it's too small, he will be reckless.

28. Secretiveness

A bump here denotes the ability to keep a confidence. An over-large bump suggests a crafty, lying character who enjoys plotting against others, while a small bump belongs to the person who cannot keep anything to himself.

29. Self-esteem

If the bump is very large the subject will be pompous and full of self-aggrandizement; if it's small, he will be self-effacing and easily pushed around.

Area D

30. Approbativeness

This concerns our status and standing in the community, as well as the amount of praise that we attract. It rules politeness and social and public relations skills. If the bump is large, the subject may be full of himself. On the other hand he may become famous, respected or an authority on a particular subject. If very small, he will be indifferent to the opinions of others and perhaps anti-social.

31. Continuity

This refers to concentration and mental application. If the bump is over-large, the subject could be obsessive. If small, he won't be able to concentrate on anything for long.

32. Constructiveness

This indicates the ability to make things, do DIY, make clothes and to be creative or artistic. A large bump here could suggest someone who is always busily engaged with some project. A small one denotes a lack of dexterity and a lack of interest in making anything.

Area E

33. Acquisitiveness

This rules the ability to earn money, obtain possessions and to obtain knowledge. Obviously, if this is over-large the subject will be a miser and someone who hoards things. He may lack honesty due to an intense desire to amass things. A small bump denotes a drifter or perhaps a subject whose values are not materialistic.

34. Alimentiveness

This bump is concerned with the connection between the brain, the sense of taste and the stomach, so it regulates the desire to eat and drink. If it's over large, the subject will be a glutton or drunkard, but if very small, he will not be interested in eating and drinking.

To quote from original Victorian sources, "Fakirs and other hermits who consider starvation to be necessary to their spiritual well-being have very small bumps of alimentiveness."

35. Execution

We call this executive ability, because it concerns the ability to create and run some kind of enterprise. There can be a destructive or revolutionary aspect to this bump that suggests that if it's over-large, the subject seeks to break down the existing status quo and impose one of his own making. A small bump here suggests an inefficient and ineffective type of person who wants peace at any price.

36. Combativeness

This bump symbolizes resistance, courage and the ability to stand up for oneself. If the bump is over large, the subject will be aggressive. If it's very small, he will be a coward.

37. Vitativeness

This rules the will to live life to the full. With a very large bump, the subject would struggle for survival against any odds, but if it's very small, he may have little tenacity and no great desire to live. Lack of a bump here could denote suicidal tendencies.

Area F

38. Friendship

This refers to the ability to be sociable and to make friends. If the bump is over large, the subject will be indiscriminate and over-friendly, but if it's small, he will be unsociable.

39. Conjugality

This concerns the ability to make lasting relationships or to make a success of marriage. A normal or large bump here shows an ability to make relationships, whereas a small one belongs to a loner.

40. Amativeness

This rules the sexual instincts. If large, the person is a sensualist. An over large bump here denotes someone who prizes sexual conquests over other forms of relationship. If it's small, obviously the subject will lack sensuality or sexual desire.

41. Inhabitiveness

This denotes a love of home life and a love of one's country. If over developed, this subject could hang on to his home at any cost, or he could make a great fuss about his home and its contents. If the bump is very small, this person may be something of a drifter with little regard for a home or even for his country.

42. Philoprogenitiveness

This means a love of and a desire for children, and a love of pets. If the bump is very large, the subject relates better to children and pets than to adults. If small, he will not be interested in either children or pets.

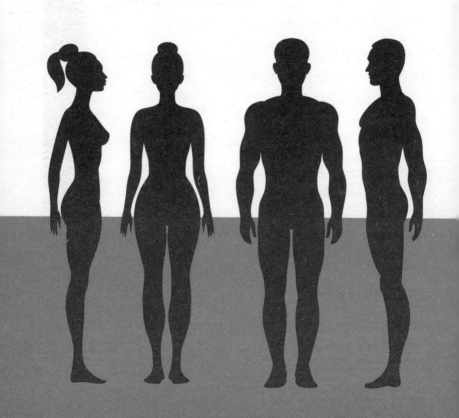

Chinese
Face Reading

3

To some extent, we all read faces all of the time. When we look at someone who is new to us, we unconsciously assess them and form opinions about them, but in addition to this instinctive form of face reading, there are far more detailed methods, with rules and regulations that have been carefully worked out over a long period of time. The best exponents of this skill are undoubtedly the Chinese, because they specialize in this form of divination. In common with all other serious forms of divination, this is a deep and difficult subject to master, but I'll just dip into the subject in order to introduce you to a fascinating skill.

Way back in the past, the school curriculum included physiognomy, along with palmistry, until the time of Henry VIII, when puritanical religions came in and outlawed these interests.

Three Major Areas of the Face

The Chinese call the forehead area down to the eyebrows Heaven, and this is associated with the early years of one's life. The middle section of the face, from the eyebrows down to the base of the nose is called Human, and this is associated with the middle years of life. The lower section, from the base of the nose down to the bottom of the face is termed Earth, and this is concerned with old age.

Any part of the face that is scarred, malformed, dented or discolored suggests a problem with the aspect of the subject's life associated with that segment of his face. Grey or black marks, whether they are a permanent feature or just a temporary situation, denote problems that are themselves either temporary or

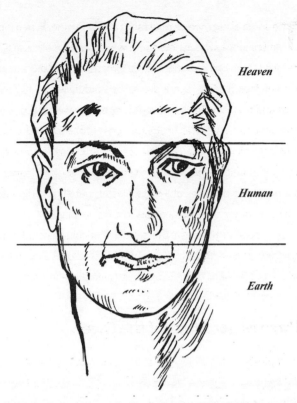

Heaven

Human

Earth

permanent depending upon the type of dark mark. Even if the discoloration is caused by a trick of the light, it will mean something to a Chinese face-reading specialist. As in every other form of divination, intuition also plays a part.

Heaven

Positive: If this area is clean, clear and well defined, the person will have a good start in life with good parents and a useful education.

Negative: Scarring, dents or discoloration here indicate a troubled childhood and a poor education. The problems will be worse for a man if the disfigurement is on the left, while for a woman if the disfigurement is on the right. A wide forehead is generally considered beneficial, but in a woman, a very wide forehead suggests poor personal relationships. The lines on the forehead offer a good deal of information, some being lucky and others unfortunate.

Human

Positive: The middle section of the subject's life will be happy and productive, with stability in relationships and success in the career.

Negative: This brings unhappiness, a lack of success at work and poor relationships. A human section longer than either of the other two sections suggests a determined and self-disciplined personality.

Earth

Positive: This indicates a happy old age with good relationships with children and grandchildren, along with prosperity and comfort.

Negative: This denotes an unhappy and poor old age.

The Thirteen Divisions of the Face

The Chinese further divide the face into 13 sub-sections. Here is a very simplified form of the 13 -section reading, starting from the top of the face and working downward.

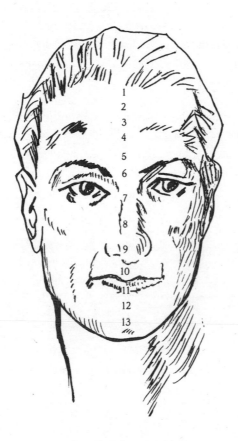

The 13 divisions of the face

1. Tien chung

If this is clean and clear, the subject will have a happy childhood and youth, a good relationship with the parents; the subject's parents will live to a ripe old age. If it's marked or misshapen, there will be unhappiness during youth, and poverty or discord in the childhood home. Veins, dark marks and so forth here suggest accidents and sudden losses of money or prestige. A widow's peak suggests that the father may die before the mother does.

2. Tien ting

This also refers to the parents and background, but it relates more to the mother than the father. Negatively, a marked area suggests that people won't believe the individual when he is telling the truth.

3. Ssu k'ung

A good complexion here suggests a fortunate and successful life, whereas discolorations tell of a bad patch in the subject's career.

4. Chung cheng

If dented, the intellect will be low. If scarred, bumpy or sporting a mole, the subject will be impatient and largely unable to bring his plans to fruition, due either to bad public relations skills or to bad luck. He will also find it hard to make and keep friends.

5. Yin t'ang

If this is healthy, the subject will receive an inheritance and he will succeed in business. Eyebrows that meet or almost meet denote failure, bad luck and a lack of respect from other people. Marks, scars and black moles can indicate anything from adoption to illness and failure, or even a term of imprisonment. Wrinkles or creases between the eyebrows are all right if the subject is over forty years of age, otherwise they denote difficulties, tension and even a jealous nature.

6. Shan gen

Grayness here denotes illness, whereas a green patch at the side indicates adultery. A mole suggests stomach problems, emigration or imprisonment!

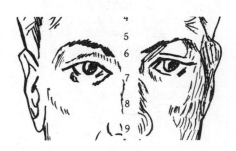

7. Men shang

Moles here suggest stomach trouble, relationship problems or possibly an ill partner. Darkness here denotes a sick child.

8. Shou shang

A high bony nose suggests failure in business. Moles and discolorations signify a sick husband and difficulties with females.

9. Chun t'ou

The tip of the nose should be full in shape and clear of marks, hairs and blackheads for good fortune.

10. Jen chung

This is the grooved area between the base of the nose and the mouth, which is called the filtrum, or the falin line. If the base of the groove is wider than the upper and the indentation neither

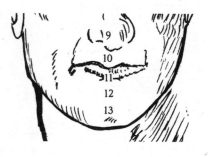

too deep nor too flat, the subject will have healthy children and will achieve a high level of wealth and status in life. If it's wider at the top and shallow, the subject will have trouble in having children. His nature will be sour and he will have bad manners. Relationships will be difficult. If this area is bent, the subject will be childless, deceitful and unpopular. A straight line marked down the middle of the groove denotes children late in life.

11. Shui hsing

The mouth should be reasonably full, with a pinkish color and upturned corners to ensure prosperity, good health and a happy marriage.

12. Ch'eng chiang

If this area is dark in the morning, the subject should avoid traveling over water during the course of that day. A man who has a hairless gap beneath his lower lip or a person of either sex who has a discoloration or scar in this area must be careful of their diet, because the stomach may be weak.

13. Ti ko

The chin should be rounded, slightly protuberant and strong in appearance. A sharp chin is unlucky and a chin that points to the side belongs to someone who holds grudges. Any scarring or discoloration denotes money losses and possibly the loss of an inheritance. This can also predict family sickness and accidents.

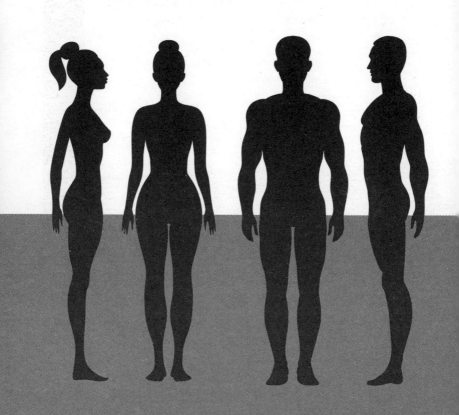

Western
Face Reading

4

In Western face reading we look at many different aspects of the face, including shape and profile, and then at individual features such as eyebrows, nose, mouth, forehead, ears, and so forth. Each of these specific facial areas has its own story to tell, and we will explore these in more depth in the following chapters. For now, let's get an overview of the shape of things.

We consider three basic face shapes, which are generally described as: round, triangular (or heart-shaped), and square (or rectangular).

Face Shapes

The round or oval face denotes a pleasant, friendly person who needs a good home and family life. He has good judgment, intuition and a desire for justice and fair play. He can work hard and he is capable, but he can also relax when necessary.

A person with a square or rectangular face is dynamic, determined and capable, strong-willed, opinionated, intelligent and tough. He has leadership qualities and physical strength. He is dexterous, good with mechanics and he would make a good soldier.

Recent tests have shown that male babies who receive an extra blast of testosterone while in the womb develop larger, more rounded heads and faces. The same goes for those with a powerful brow and jaw line. These people make uncompromising sportsmen, as they are far more aggressive than their softer-featured teammates. Those with a square jaw love to fight, so they may become boxers or wrestlers or join the armed forces—or they may become football hooligans or some other kind of anti-social nuisance.

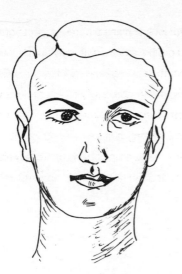

Round or oval-shaped face

Triangular-shaped face

Square-shaped face

A triangular or heart-shaped face shows that the person is sensitive, creative and intellectual. He has a good mind and a good memory. He can be hard to understand due to moodiness. He is a dreamer who needs direction in life, and this isn't helped because he is restless and easily bored.

Each of these three face shapes can also be interpreted in combination. People will often have a face shape that is a blending of two types.

Round/triangular face

This person is intellectual and businesslike, but also restless and moody. He can be over-optimistic and over-confident at times, and he finds honest self-assessment hard.

Round/square face

This individual is active, cheerful, opinionated and egotistical, but he is also capable and businesslike.

Square/triangular face

This person is clever, impetuous, inventive and active. He can prosper as a result of creativity.

Within each of these three face shapes we also consider width and depth. For example, a round face can be a long oval, or a shorter circle shape.

Narrow faces

Narrow faces belong to those who follow rather than lead, and who have to learn confidence later in life. They are anxious and self-conscious, insecure and fearful. They fit in with others rather than trying to force others to fit in with their preferences.

Broad faces

This type of face belongs to those who are determined, independent, decisive, self-sufficient and able to take charge of others. They stand up for themselves if threatened or challenged, often being aggressive when there is no need for it.

Profiles

The concave face

This individual is steady and rather inflexible. He appears deep and clever, but may not be so. He wastes time fiddling about with minor matters. He is reserved, interested in the past, and has a good memory.

The convex face

This person is a good communicator. He is lively, clever, quick-thinking. He talks and he gets things done, but he is a poor listener. He is practical, quick-on-the-uptake and active, but he quickly becomes bored and restless.

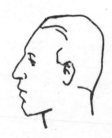

The straight face

This person is calm, deliberate, reasonable, with the patience to work things out thoroughly, but also stubborn, tenacious, and strongly opinionated. I've noticed that many actors of both sexes have this kind of profile, often with a straighter forehead than in this illustration.

Hair

I've talked about hair earlier in this book, but here is a bit more hairy folklore.

- Fine hair belongs to someone who thinks quickly, is upset by loud talk, sweeping gestures or drunken people. He feels minor changes in atmosphere and temperature, and is sensitive to taste, touch and the environment. He likes quality rather than quantity.
- Coarse hair belongs to those who respond slowly, and who may be loud and boisterous. They want a lot of everything and don't always know when to stop. They like pastimes like camping, soldiering and being uncomfortable. They don't notice heat, cold or changes in the environment.

Forehead

If the forehead is well proportioned and free of marks, scars and discoloration, the person will have a good start in life and a good relationship with his parents.

- A large forehead suggests a deep thinker, and a narrow forehead an analytical thinker.
- A forehead that is flat or dented inward suggests good concentration and a cautious temperament, while one that bulges outward suggests shrewdness and good powers of observation.
- A low forehead denotes a nature that is practical rather than intellectual.

Eyebrows

- Clean, clear, gently curving eyebrows indicate refinement, humor, intelligence and a lucky life.
- Curved eyebrows suggest an inquiring mind and arched ones, a creative imagination.
- Bushy eyebrows belong to a more temperamental, somewhat unpleasant type. Very unruly brows denote an unconventional and freewheeling mind that sees all around a problem but who may lack tact and get into arguments. He may do nothing until his mid-thirties and then make a success of himself.
- Very thin eyebrows suggest a fussy nature.
- Upward sloping eyebrows denote ambition.
- Tufted eyebrows indicate pleasure in hurting others.
- Downwardly sloping brows suggest a lack of energy and a tendency to whine.
- Widely spaced eyebrows show refinement and adaptability.
- Closely spaced eyebrows denote a hot temper, energy, and determination, but also indicate a busy person who tends to worry about everything. He needs to relax and stop taking things personally or he will become angry and depressed.
- When the brows are thick at the starting point, the person jumps to conclusions.
- Straight eyebrows endow logic, but lack feelings.
- Curved eyebrows endow sensitivity and feeling, but lack logic.
- Angled, tent-shaped eyebrows belong to good supervisors.
- High eyebrows denote a certain amount of secretiveness; the type of person who stands back and observes others, and who needs his own space and time in which to do things. He may

be unfriendly and aloof—a stand-offish personality who knows it all and who isn't interested in others.
- Low eyebrows belong on those who talk about their ideas. They make friends easily, they like to be informal and while they can keep their distance, they are open to and accessible to others.

Eyes

The eyes are considered the most important feature, and "good" eyes can mitigate the effects of other "bad" features.
- Eyes that dart about restlessly may belong to a dishonest person, and someone who won't meet your eye is deemed to be cunning.
- Crows' feet around the eyes in an older person suggest the ability to solve problems, while in a young person they denote laziness.
- A person who has no fold in the eyelid will overreact to emotional situations.
- A subject whose eyes bulge with the white showing all around the iris has a thyroid problem.
- Oval eyes suggest a good temper and a sharp mind, while rounded ones show a naive and trusting nature.
- Hooded eyes indicate a suspicious and secretive nature, as do narrowed eyes.
- Eyes that are wide apart signify openness and tolerance, while eyes that are close together suggest intolerance and a tough attitude to oneself and to others.

- Protruding eyes denote creativity but laziness, and deep-set eyes indicate tenacity, but a lack of creativity.
- Vertical worry lines between the eyes shows that the person pushes himself hard and that his standards may be too high.
- A horizontal line shows that the person is carrying a heavy burden and needs to find ways of reducing his responsibilities and his level of stress.
- Widely set eyes show tolerance and an ability to judge the outcome to a situation, but these people are gullible. They cannot tolerate changes and upsets well and they become over-emotional when faced with difficulties.
- Deep-set eyes suggest caution and reserve. These people are romantic, but also realistic about relationships. They make a success of themselves once they have passed their mid-thirties.
- Protruding eyes belong to quite difficult people who may be clever and artistic, but who don't make the best use of their talents. They are envious of others, strong-willed and bigheaded, and they hate being interrupted or ignored.

Ears

- High ears process information fast.
- Low ears need time to process information, but once they make their minds up, these people don't budge.
- Long ears indicate long life—but the ears tend to keep growing slightly throughout life, so they do get longer as one gets older.
- When the outer ring of the ear is far from the inner ring, the person is practical, but he also keeps thoughts to himself.

- Sticking-out ears belong to a thinker and scholar who is an independent thinker and unconventional, non-conformist. He is also stubborn and determined.
- A vertical line on the earlobes denotes possible heart trouble and a person's need to take more care of his health.
- When the earlobes are attached to the side of the head, the person is bossy.

Nose

- A small ball on the end of the nose means artistic talent and an appreciation of art, quality, music and beauty.
- A bulbous nose belongs to a collector who knows the value of goods and who needs money in the bank.
- Prominent noses belong to those who think a lot of themselves and who look down on others. These people lose their tempers and can become nasty if they aren't treated with respect, or if they can't get their own way.

Mouth

- Convention says that someone with a mouth that turns upward is optimistic, prepared to hear and think the best of others, and very sociable. My experience of such people is that they tend to be the opposite.
- Convention also says that the downward-turning mouth belongs to a pessimist who distrusts everything he hears and who expects to be disappointed in life. Folklore also says that

this person will make a success of his life after he has reached his mid-forties. My experience is that those who have a strong Saturn or an emphasis on the sign of Capricorn on their horoscope have this kind of mouth. These people are hard-working, status conscious, ambitious, easily offended and unwilling to help those outside their immediate family. They aren't particularly pessimistic, but they definitely do make headway in life once they start to hit middle age.

Teeth

- A space between the teeth belongs to someone with a great sense of humor and a certain amount of luck in life. This person can be indecisive.
- Two large front teeth symbolize impatience, obstinacy and a need for reassurance.

Chin

- A cleft chin indicates stubbornness and sometimes business ability.
- A pointed chin shows a bossy person who may push his or her partner around. This person is oversensitive and moody, and he hates being told what to do.
- A receding chin often occurs when Mercury or the sign of Gemini is a major feature on a person's horoscope, and it shows a talent for speaking, communicating and writing. This person hates conflict, so he fits in with others and is a

peacemaker. This is seen as weakness by others, so they bully him. This tends to backfire, because the "apparently" weak person often does much better in life than the bully. However, success comes as a result of a combination of natural talent and lucky breaks, because the person doesn't plan his life or make enough effort to get on. He never expects others to fall in with his plans (if he actually makes any) and he goes with the flow, all of which leads to poverty in later life.

Mannerisms

Mannerisms can also be considered as part of the subject of body language (which we'll look at more specifically in chapter 10). However, no body part can really be considered in absence of its movement. Here are some of the most basic mannerisms you will notice.

- Those who bite their nails are unhappy about their lives, but don't have the strength or courage to change their situation or walk away from it. They do what others want them to do, and become depressed, lacking in direction and somewhat lost. They lack focus and they can become impatient.
- Those who rub their noses suffer from allergies.
- People who rub their chins are living in a difficult situation that they haven't created and they don't have a trusted friend in whom they can confide. They lose confidence and courage as a result.
- People whose head or shoulders sag have problems that they can't solve and whatever they do, the situation tends to become

worse. They become introverted, shy, sad and pessimistic.

- Those who tap their feet when their partner is speaking are showing that they don't agree with the opinions they are hearing. They become impatient with others, or even envious of them.

- Those who tap their fingers feel that nothing is happening quickly enough for them. They may be waiting for someone to arrive or to do something for them. They become mistrustful and cold.

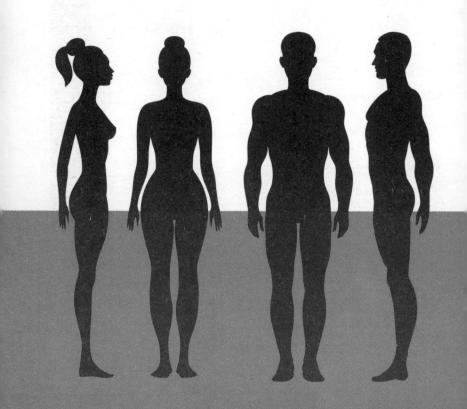

A Closer Look at the Face

5

The two features most immediately noticed when you look at someone's face are the eyes and teeth. Let's take a moment to look at both in more detail.

Eyes

Iridology is the science of diagnosing illness by studying small marks and imperfections in the eye. Some conditions that affect the appearance of the eyes are quite well known. For instance, jaundice will turn the white of the eye yellow, and anemia can be spotted by pulling down the lower lid and checking that the color is pink rather than pale gray. Red eyes can denote fatigue or too many nights on the tiles. An iridologist will be able to tell you about specific health problems. However, I'll now concentrate on the eyes in connection with the personality. The information for this section of this book was given to me by Madelene McConomy, a professional iridologist.

Streams, flowers, and jewels

The stream eye has fibers in the iris, radiating outward from the pupil in relatively orderly rows. This belongs to an introverted per-

son who is slightly withdrawn and highly sensitive. This person is responsive to changes in the weather, changes in his body, and is also sensitive to the moods of others. He is intuitive and he may be psychic, but he is also accustomed to using logic and intelligence. It's easy to hurt this type of person, but hard to lie to him or to butter him up as he sees (or rather feels) right through to the truth. His most acute sense is that of touch.

The flower eye has an attractive kaleido-scopic effect caused by the fibers parting and rejoining to form "petals" around the iris. This person can express his emotional needs with ease. He acts on impulse and is something of a go-getter. This subject is strongly affected by the appearance of things and will feel unhappy working or living in unpleasant sur-roundings. His most acute sense is that of sight.

The jewel eye has patches of dense color that look like jewels upon a velvet tray. The jewel type is withdrawn and intellectual. He relies upon logic and is most comfortable when sifting ideas in his head. He appears cool and introverted because he finds it dif-ficult to express emotion, and he may deny the intuitive side of his personality. His strongest response is to sound, so he may be disconcerted by discordant noise or soothed by quiet music, and he may pick up useful information from the radio or teaching discs.

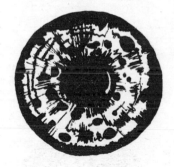

Many people are combinations of all these types, but usually the stream, flower or jewel motif predominates. People whose eyes are predominantly of one type are often attracted to those who have one of the other two types.

Left and right eyes

Here is an interesting exercise that you can easily try for yourself.

Establish which is your dominant eye. This will be the one with the densest or most colorful iris, and that is the side of the face that corresponds to the side of the body you lie on when you are asleep.

- If the right eye is dominant, you will be masculine in outlook, preferring to live and work in a well-defined hierarchy and with the ability to organize yourself and others. You will be sociable, outgoing and interested in working among groups of people.
- If the left eye predominates, your outlook will be feminine. You will be instinctively responsive to the needs of others, and you will be cooperative and diplomatic. You will value your home and your privacy and will wish to nurture and to be nurtured within a family environment.
- Right eye dominants are attracted to left eye dominants and vice versa.
- It's also interesting to note that right eye dominants are more attached to their fathers while left eye dominants are more attached to their mothers.
- Right eyes denote characteristics inherited from the father and left ones from the mother.
- Even if the relationship between the person and his parents isn't a particularly happy one, the rule remains the same—the right eye relates to the father and the left eye relates to the mother.

Other considerations for the eye

- A ring effect located around the outer edge of iris away denotes an extroverted achiever who likes to get out and about, to meet his pals in the pub and to work and play in a group setting. This type is competitive and possibly sporty.
- A ring close to the pupil belongs to an introvert who prefers to work things out for himself. He needs time alone and he isn't especially competitive. He has a natural ability to understand the motives of others and can see things objectively.
- A particularly dense stream eye with no ring belongs to a super-sensitive, intuitive, introvert who prefers to tread an inward path through life.
- The eyes record a shock to the system resulting from, for instance, a broken bone, but they don't register operations carried out under anesthetic.
- Sparkling clear whites of the eye denote good health, but can also show a selfish personality, unconcerned about the needs of others.
- A plethora of tiny red veins belongs to a person who spends his life surrounded by many other people.
- A dark gap in the iris shaped like a keyhole means that the subject has a really bad relationship with one of his parents (right for dad, left for mum) which, if not resolved, will result in phobias or even physical illness.

Teeth

Difficulties before and during birth will cause the tips of the permanent (secondary) teeth to develop badly, because secondary
teeth begin to form and calcify even before birth. In the case of a
particularly difficult birth, the tips of these second teeth will show
signs of hypo-calcification, which means insufficient calcification,
so their ultimate development will be poor. Severe childhood illness may leave a mark in the form of a horizontal dent across
all the teeth at the point at which they were in their growth and
development at the time of the illness. This linear dent will show
up later as a staggered dent across all the teeth. This is very like
the lateral dents that appear across fingernails as a result of a
shock to the system after someone has an illness or a severe emotional upset.

Lifestyles and problems that damage teeth

- Heavy use of antibiotics, especially Tetracycline, can leave
  the teeth with a blue-gray, gray-green or yellowish-brown
  appearance.
- Too much fluoride can cause spotting and mottling.
- Tea, coffee and some foods stain the teeth, but the greatest
  source of grunge on the teeth comes from smoking, while the
  acid left on the teeth from smoking damages them badly.
- Pipe smokers sometimes wear down the tips of their incisors
  where they habitually grip their pipes. Over-consumption of cit-
  rus fruits, especially grapefruit, can cause permanent damage.
- Some people grind their teeth, especially during sleep. This

nervous habit not only damages the teeth, but can also be a cause of migraine.

- Those who hold pins or tacks in their teeth as part of their job develop characteristic notches.
- Boxers and other fighters can damage their teeth.

Spacing of teeth

- Defective spacing of teeth is mainly congenital and is the result of the genetic melting pot from which most of us spring. Natives of the Amazon and African tribesmen have teeth and jaws that are entirely compatible. Their teeth fit together neatly, thus reducing the chance of tooth decay. The ill-matched teeth of urbanized races encourage the entrapment of foods and the start of decay.
- People who have a gap in their front teeth seem to be sociable and humorous, and they often work for, with or in front of the public in some way. Their breezy manner belies a hard-working perfectionist who can actually be irritable and difficult to live with.
- A pointy overbite seems to belong to an intelligent, but shy person who covers up a slight lack of confidence with wit and humor.
- People with inward-leaning incisors are selfish, anti-social and they don't mind hurting others when the mood is upon them.

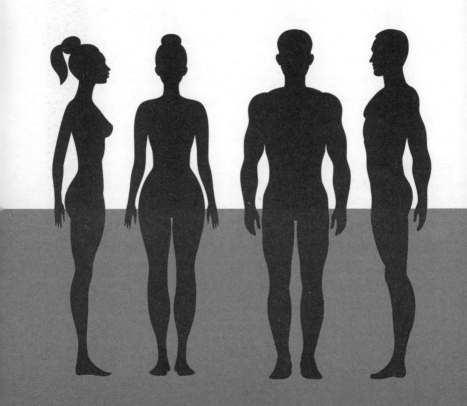

Hands

6

Ahand reader can explore a client's character and personality in great depth; he can also discern many events of the client's past and see trends for his future. This knowledge, added to good counseling skills, enables the reader to advise clients about their future paths and choices. Lines and marks on the hands change from time to time, and they can change quite rapidly when one makes a life-changing decision. It's worth taking a print of your own hand now and comparing it with another taken in six month's time. The easy way to do this is to smear very bright or dark colored lipstick on the hand and then press a piece of paper onto the hand. Peel it off carefully, date the page, and leave it to dry.

There are limitations to palmistry, just as there are with every other form of divination. Palmists have the advantage of being able to look at the whole of a client's life at once, so they aren't limited to one segment of it. However, this makes it impossible to answer questions of an immediate nature, such as, "Will I get a new job soon?" It's often useful to do a hand reading and then follow it up with another type of reading, such as tarot cards.

Left and Right Hands

The dominant hand is the one with which you write. Some palmists say that the minor hand is the one that shows what we want, while the dominant hand shows what we get. Others say that the dominant hand outlines the future while the minor one chronicles the past. In many cases, the underlying personality is on the minor hand, while the dominant one shows adaptation to circumstances. Health matters and things that affect the emotions are often easier to see on the minor hand, while business matters and the parts of our lives that we live outside the house are clearer on the major one.

People with large hands take their time about things. They are thorough and unhurried in their pace of work and they also display perseverance in other areas of their lives, but they can't think on their feet or make on the spot decisions. Small-handed people are much quicker in their responses, either by being speedy in all that they do or by being quick to adapt and change.

Hard hands belong to hard workers, while soft hands belong to those who like to coddle themselves. However, we have to be sure that the hands are not reflecting situations such as illness, pregnancy or vegetarianism. Fleshy hands suggest self-indulgence while a mass of thick, hard-packed flesh belongs on the hands of those who want their own way at all costs.

Shape

- Square hands indicate practicality and long square hands indicate an ability to handle detailed work.
- Rounded hands belong to emotional people who are more inclined to look for happiness in relationships than in competitive situations. Such people like variety in their lives and enjoy socializing.
- Bony, spatulate hands have finger ends that splay outward and which may incline toward the index finger. These people are competitive for themselves and on behalf of their families. They cannot be controlled or dominated by others. They sometimes relate more easily to animals than to other human beings.

- Knobby hands are a sign of caution and reserve, but also of intellectualism and an enquiring, scientific mind. These people like to plan their lives and don't like changes.
- Smooth hands indicate refinement and sometimes laziness.

Color

- Pale hands denote a circulatory problem.
- Yellow hands suggest jaundice.
- Red hands may indicate high blood pressure, a thyroid condition, pressure on the lungs from heavy smoking or simply an inherited tendency toward this kind of redness.

If the hands are especially hot, cold, wet or dry, the client may have a health problem at the time of the reading and this could affect the internal organs.

Thumbs

- A well-developed thumb adds strength to the character, while a weak, floppy one denotes a weak personality.
- An overlarge thumb with a wide and heavy-looking ball shows a tendency to ride roughshod over others.
- If a large thumb is low set (a lower joining to the hand) and turns back at the ball, this person is restless. He may be good at acting, either on stage or television or in his work in some other way, perhaps as a salesperson. He can also be impulsive and strange about money, being stingy some of the time and spending money like water at others.

- A high-set thumb (joined higher up the hand) shows inhibition, caution, shyness and a desire for stability. These people are more interested in staying put than in moving around, and they prefer mental activities to physical ones.
- A large joint at the base of the thumb shows the ability to solve practical problems, so this person might be a good engineer, builder or farmer.
- A large, low joint on a wide hand shows an interest in sport.

Fingers

Each finger has its own meaning, so you must use your own judgment as to which of the fingers predominates. You should consider for each its length and position.
- Long fingers mean artistic ability, attention to detail and sensitivity.
- Short fingers suggest energy, action and a fairly tough-minded attitude to life.
- Fingers that lean toward the index finger suggest independence.
- Fingers that cling together indicate a need for direction and guidance from others.

The index finger
Palmists call this the Jupiter finger.

A well-developed index finger belongs to a subject with a well-developed ego. He is independent, self-motivated and has established views, formed early in life. He may have leadership qualities or he may just be bossy. If the finger is pointed, he has some pretty rigid religious views as well.

If the index finger is short or weak looking, the individual lacks self-confidence and may lean on others, hoping that they will make his decisions for him. In some cases, the finger is actually a good length, but it's set low on the hand, and this shows that the individual develops confidence later in life while retaining a diplomatic and cooperative nature.

The middle finger

Palmists call this the Saturn finger.

Most people have a well-developed middle finger, which suggests strong survival instincts, a need for financial and emotional security and an ability to deal with the practicalities of life.

If the base phalange is full, the subject needs material security and comfort.

If it's thin, he may reach outward for spiritual and intellectual achievement rather than material gain.

If this finger is short or if it looks weak, the subject lacks endurance and he is unable to stick to anything. He is also reluctant to stretch his mind. He relies on others to fulfill his material and spiritual needs.

The ring finger

Palmists call this the Apollo finger.

If the finger is long and well developed, the subject has good taste. He needs pleasant surroundings and beautiful objects around him. He is creative, imaginative and possibly artistic, displaying a good sense of line and balance in all that he does. His home and family are important to him. At work, he needs job-satisfaction as much as he needs material gain.

If the base phalange is full, he may want to work with objects of beauty, whereas if it's thin, he will be drawn to the world of ideals and ideas.

A short ring finger suggests a messy person, uninterested in aesthetics. He may not care about having a nice home, and if he bothers to work, it will be purely for the money and not for the satisfaction of doing a good job of work. He will avoid any form of gambling in business or in life, partly because he lacks imagination.

The little finger
Palmists call this the Mercury finger.

This finger is associated with all forms of communication, so if it's well developed, the subject will be a good speaker and writer, and possibly a confident salesperson. He will be interested in relating to others both socially and sexually.

If the Mercury finger is stunted, the individual is shy or withdrawn and unable to express himself easily. He may have only one or two basic interests in life, and he may be unable to co-operate with others or to understand their needs. He may be uninterested in sex or too shy and inhibited to form a relationship.

Finger Gesture

The way that people place their fingers while using their hands gives quite a few clues as to their characters.

Thumbs open at an angle of 90 degrees or more indicate friendly, gossipy types who express their feelings fairly easily.

Those whose thumbs are pitched higher on the hand with a tighter opening angle are introverted and rather shy. These subjects are apt to hide their real feelings, and they can keep the secrets of others.

When the index finger pulls away from the other fingers, the person is independent and he arranges his lifestyle and his environment to suit himself. He will resist anyone who tries to control or dominate him.

If the index finger clings to the middle finger, the subject will cling to his family, and look for approval from others. This type of subject has the capacity to learn from experience, so he may well develop a stronger, more independent personality as time goes on. He is also likely to be a hard and dedicated worker—possibly because he unconsciously seeks approval and praise.

Saturn and Apollo fingers clinging together

A gap between the middle and ring fingers suggests rebelliousness, either openly expressed through difficult behavior or subtly expressed through withdrawal and self-centeredness.

If the two middle fingers cling together, the individual needs a secure home life, job satisfaction and he needs a hobby that gives him artistic or creative fulfillment. Some palmists see this as an indication of guilt feelings, but I'm not so sure about this.

When the little finger pulls away from the ring finger, the person likes his home to be quiet and private. He is independent and he likes to make up his own mind and to have his own opinions. He is hard to persuade and influence. He likes to organize his own life and he needs time alone, to think and to recharge his mental batteries. In some indefinable way, he withdraws himself from others in order to protect his independence. This is also an indication of people who distance themselves sexually, and who may choose a celibate life rather than to be encumbered by relationships and all that they entail.

Mercury finger pulling away

Fingertips

- Full, fat, hard-packed fingertips show a fighter who will live life his way regardless of the cost.
- Heavy fingertips belong to a person who lacks diplomacy and who is unlikely to compromise. This person has great physical and mental strength.
- Very heavy finger ends suggest either a lumpish personality who will never achieve anything (and doesn't want to) or a coarse, uncouth type of person.
- Soft, flat fingertips denote a soft, undemanding personality who will usually try to fit into most circumstances and tend to avoid confrontation wherever possible.

- Formations known as "droplets" denote a well-developed sense of touch. These are usually found on the hands of a subject who is clever with his or her hands, so this feature is often associated with dressmaking and other craftwork.
- Long fingertips suggest academic ability, and they certainly show an active mind.

Fingerprints

After looking at the general shape of the fingertips, look at the fingerprints and see what you can find.

The most common shape is the loop. This suggests sociability and the ability to work as part of a team, or to co-operate as a family member. The subject needs to give and receive affection and he is kind-hearted and emotional.

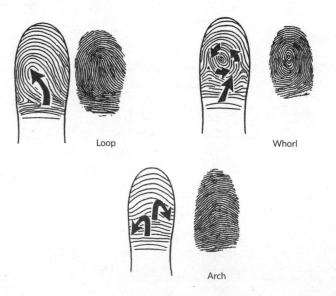

Loop

Whorl

Arch

The whorl suggests independence. If this only appears on one or two fingers, the subject may have a talent for whatever is associated with that finger. If there are whorls on the full set of fingers, the subject will either achieve great things or he will never get anything off the ground.

Arches show shyness and hesitancy. These are usually found on the index or middle fingers. They show that the subject will have to suffer or struggle in some area of his life. Many arches denote a person who lacks confidence and energy. Much the same goes for arches on the index fingers.

The Peacock's Eye

The peacock's eye is a whorl with a kind of elongated tail that curves slightly and it brings artistic or creative ability to whatever finger it's on. I have one on one of my little fingers, and I am obviously a good writer. A palmistry friend called Robin Lown has one on one of his middle fingers, and he is an excellent carpenter.

Double loops

Double loops or composite whorls show indecisiveness, but they can also show intuition. It's as though the gut feelings and logical mind aren't always saying the same thing.

Warts

My palmist friend, Malcolm Wright, once explained his theories to me on the significance of warts on the hands. Since then, I've verified his ideas by chatting to various wart-laden people. The idea is that a wart on the back of the hand represents a problem caused by others, while one on the palm side represents a blockage or a problem that may or may not have been created by the subject, but that only he can resolve. If you have a wart and want to know which area of your life it represents, look at the map of the hand below and then refer to the relevant section in this chapter. For example, a wart on the index finger would imply some blockage affecting your self-esteem and decision-making abilities. Whether this is due to the behavior of someone close to you, or to lack of courage on your part, will depend upon whether the wart is, respectively, on the back or front of the finger.

The Map of the Hand

The map of the hand is divided into locations called mounts. Many of these so-called mounts are more like valleys, but they provide a useful guide to the geography of the hand. Any mount that seems to predominate will show an area of life particularly important to the subject, while lines and marks that touch the various mounts show how the subject's personality, interests, energies and instincts are expressed. The positioning of lines and marks that cross or touch the various mounts offer clues as to the subject's future.

The mount of Jupiter

A well-developed Jupiter mount suggests ambition, a strong ego and idealism. A cross here suggests marriage to a successful partner, while a square denotes executive or teaching ability. A very

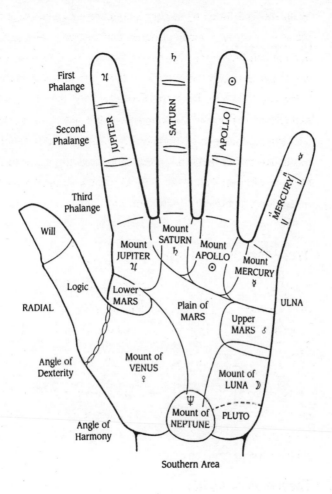

The map of the hand

high mount indicates a desire for money, status and power, while a flat one suggests a lack of ambition and a desire for a peaceful life.

The mount of Saturn

This is usually a valley rather than a mount. This area is concerned with money and security, along with a person's aims and ambitions. It can symbolize the direction of the subject's interests, especially later in life. Lines that reach this area suggest success as a result of hard work, but possibly a slightly dour attitude to life. The old-time books state that a cross here suggests death by hanging, but I haven't found any truth in that idea, although a colleague suggests that the subject might have contemplated murdering someone at some time in his life!

The mount of Apollo

This area is concerned to some extent with one's home and family. It also shows hobbies and interests, especially creative ones. Vertical lines in this area suggests happiness in old age, while a cross can show a win or some other kind of unearned income. I've noticed small crosses here in the hands of writers, because while they definitely earn their income, it can keep coming along for several years in the form of royalties.

The mount of Mercury

A well-developed Mercury mount suggests communications ability, or nursing or healing ability and an interest in people. A cross here shows the ability to deal with machinery, including computers and other communications equipment, while a square will show some kind of misunderstanding or temporary lack of communication with someone close to the subject. Three slightly diagonal lines here, possibly scored through by a fourth, show healing ability. This healing touch may be expressed in normal medical and nursing terms, or in the form of spiritual healing. It can even be expressed by a subject who takes care of animals. The outer edge of this area offers information about relationships and children, as we will see later in this chapter.

The mounts of Mars

Lower Mars (the one near the thumb) shows military or paramilitary interests. I've seen a well-developed Mars Mount on the hands of scout leaders, police officers, paramedical types and even canteen managers. This mount shows organizational skill and the ability to work within a team.

Upper Mars is found on the percussion edge of the hand. If well developed, this mount indicates endurance and the ability to cope with anything, without being shocked or upset. This suggests the ability to recuperate easily from illness and the strength to withstand pressure from others. An over-developed Mars shows an aggressive and hot-tempered nature. Lines and marks on Upper Mars that don't reach the percussion edge can indicate some kind of mental or physical battle with which the subject has to cope at some time during his life.

Lines that curl around any part of the percussion edge, apart from those found immediately beneath the Mercury finger and above the heart line, usually relate to travel or to dealings with other countries for business purposes.

The mount of Venus

If the mount of Venus is well developed, it shows a love of home and family and a sensual nature. It may show a tendency to over eat for comfort's sake. It also shows a passion for music, art, travel and for life in general. It can show a high sex drive, and a need for frequent sex. It can also show a passion for one's job, hobbies or for anything that the person loves to do.

Lines on the edge of the hand can show help that comes from others, but they can also show obstacles placed in the subject's way. Lines that shadow the lifeline show friends and a strong connection to other members of the family. They also denote physical strength and good powers of recovery from illness.

Horizontal lines that cut through the life line and extend out into the hand suggest problems connected to the home and family.

The mount of Luna

If this mount is well developed, the subject loves to travel. He may travel around the country with his work, he may travel around the world with his work, or he may just love to travel and explore. He may live abroad at some time in his life. Luna can also denote a fondness for the outdoor life, dancing, sports or some other form of movement.

This area is associated with creativity and imagination, so if it's well developed, it shows good imaginative powers and also intuition, a good memory and the ability to understand other people. An intuition line that runs into this area shows psychic ability.

The mount of Neptune

This is a kind of bridge between the conscious mind and the material world, as represented by the two adjoining mounts (Luna and Venus). If the area is high, the subject will have a good link between these two worlds and he will be able to bring intuition and imagination to bear on his decisions. If the area is more like a valley than a ridge, the subject may be unable or unwilling to consider anything other than what he can see, hear and touch.

Lines on the Hand

This is the aspect of palmistry that everyone understands, as reading the lines is supposed to show what will happen in our lives, and the lines often do just that.

The life line

If the life line is smooth, unmarked and unbroken, the subject's life will run smoothly, while interruptions to the course of the line suggest challenges and problems that have to be overcome.

A long "island" or a doubling of the line somewhere along its course means that the subject sets his own immediate desires aside in favor of some other priority, such as the needs of a family or a course of study. When the time comes for the subject to take up the reins of his life again, a branch line may be thrown upward.

Gaps in the line suggest trauma, illness or even a period during which the subject was forced to live among people he didn't like.

A fat, curving line belongs to an energetic person who is both competitive and materialistic. This subject needs a secure

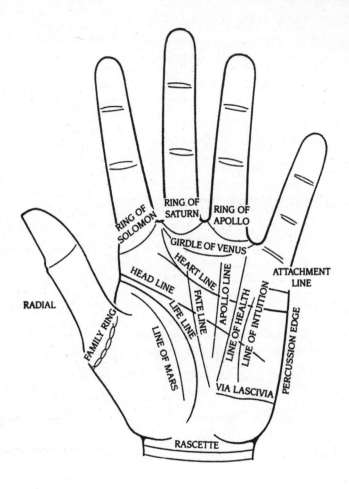

The major lines of the hand

emotional base from which to launch himself, which is why he keeps close control of his home and family.

A narrower curve suggests idealism and values that are intellectual and spiritual rather than physical and material.

A line that travels out into the hand denotes a career person. Such a person may also be drawn to people and faraway places, both in terms of actual distance and/or a different outlook from the one that was around him during his childhood.

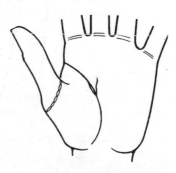

An island represents some kind of setback or loss, and if it's followed by a small rising line, this shows that the individual will take steps to improve the situation.

A setback followed by a fresh start

A short or broken life line shows some kind of enforced change of direction; it's rarely an indication of severe illness or early death! The lifeline in the illustration below is typical of the kind of enforced change in life that comes from divorce or a sudden change of career.

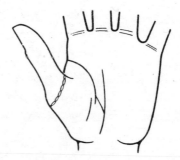

The head line

A short life line suggests major change

The head line runs across the middle of the hand. It may be straight or curved. It shows how the subject's mind works and gives a good deal of information about his career.

Long head lines belong to someone with a range of interests and good concentration.

Short ones belong to those who specialize in one particular interest, and who can only understand the world in terms of that interest. In some cases, this kind of line can be found on the hand of a businessman or woman who is skilled at delegating boring day-to-day tasks to others.

A straight head line denotes a practical and rather selfish outlook, while a curved one suggests an imaginative and more kindly one.

Wavy head lines show uneven progress in career matters with the dips in the line showing periods of depression or times when the person switches off mentally. A course of education or training will lift the head line, as will a time of forging ahead in a job.

Setbacks are shown by bars, islands and breaks in the line, while improvements are shown by branches that rise up from the line.

A long island or a patch of chaining denotes a time when the subject feels trapped in a situation that doesn't really suit him.

Forks on the line typically show versatility and communications ability.

A branch upward shows business acumen that can be expected to lead to success, while a downward branch shows intuition and an ability to communicate ideas to other people. A fork indicates writing ability.

The heart line

The heart line shows how a subject feels and how he expresses emotion.

A long heart line shows deep feelings and an ability to care for others. If it's curved, the subject will be more outwardly emotional and more inclined to express his feelings, while a straight line suggests someone who broods, sulks and keeps his hurts to himself.

The subject with a curved line will be drawn to anyone who shows him affection, while the person with the straight heart line is cautious and fussy in his choice of partner.

If the heart line is short, the subject is not really a relater. He needs others to fulfill something lacking in his own life, but he isn't really interested in the needs and the feelings of others.

Islands in the line normally show shocks and upsets in the love life. A broken line would suggest a broken heart.

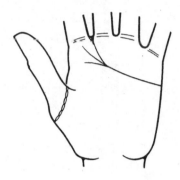

A branched heart line

If the line reaches the mount of Jupiter, the subject will want to be associated with people he can respect and admire, while also wanting to be respected and admired himself.

If the line curves tightly upward to end at the base of the fingers, the subject may be possessive or on the receiving end of someone else's possessiveness.

A triple branch on the heart line suggests a need for love, friendship, companionship and mental stimulation as well as sexual satisfaction. That's not much to ask, is it?

Attachment lines

Attachment lines appear on the edge of the hand beneath the Mercury finger, and they offer a good deal of information about a subject's relationships. They can be deceptive though, for they tend to change as the years go by. Hands don't show marriage certificates—they show feelings; therefore a particularly strong line may indicate an important relationship outside, or in place of, marriage, while a marriage that turns out to be unimportant may hardly show up at all!

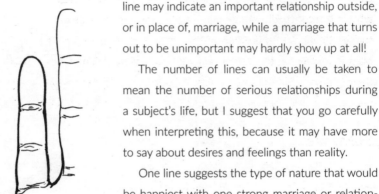

The number of lines can usually be taken to mean the number of serious relationships during a subject's life, but I suggest that you go carefully when interpreting this, because it may have more to say about desires and feelings than reality.

One line suggests the type of nature that would be happiest with one strong marriage or relationship. If this relationship ends for any reason, it will be replaced as soon as possible by another equally strong attachment.

Attachment lines

Two lines suggest that the subject would certainly consider leaving a partner if things didn't work out. This ability to break away from a partnership often does result in at least two deep relationships during one lifetime.

- Generally speaking, the lowest line is seen as the first relationship, with other ones coming afterwards.
- An attachment line that droops downward symbolizes an unhappy or unsatisfactory relationship, especially if it droops down to the heart line.

- Islands and breaks show times of trouble and unhappiness.
- Branches that travel upward show happiness, but most of all they show that the partner is doing well at work or in life.

Child lines

The very fine lines which cut through the attachment lines vertically refer to children. These can be deceptive, because people who look after children or animals often display these lines even though they have no children of their own. If there are no child lines, it's likely that the person will not have children. Sometimes there are lines but still no children; in this case, there will have been miscarriages or failed attempts to have children through IVF.

Sibling lines

There are lines that are similar to the attachment lines on the other side of the hand under the Jupiter finger, and these can tell us about brothers, sisters, other relatives of one's own generation or close friends. Fine lines that cut vertically through these attachment lines may refer to nephews and nieces, but this needs more research.

Travel lines

Travel lines appear on the percussion edge of the hand on the mounts of upper Mars, Luna, and Pluto. If they touch the head or the fate line, they indicate travel in connection with business. If these lines touch the lifeline, the subject will have friends or family in other countries. A skilled palmist can pick out the parts of the world to which a subject is likely to travel by the position of these lines.

The Fate Line

If there is no fate line, the subject is probably perfectly happy with his situation in life and under no pressure to make an effort to please others. He may be lazy and unmotivated or simply contented with his lot. If any part of the fate line appears on the hand, there will be a time of striving, achievement and success at that time of the subject's life.

Read the fate line up from the bottom of the hand. Lines that enter the fate line show important people coming into the person's life. If a line enters from the percussion side, the influential

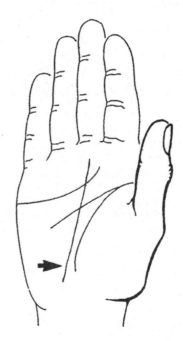

The fate line

person will be an outsider, but if it enters from the thumb side, the person may have been known to the subject and his family for some time beforehand.

Lines that cross the fate line from the thumb side show interference by parents, in-laws or other members of the family.

A strong clear fate line shows a strong sense of self. If the line travels toward Jupiter (see line d), it shows ambition, idealism and a desire for political influence.

If it travels toward Saturn (see line c), it shows a desire for material benefits, a love of land and property and an ability to cope with analysis and detail.

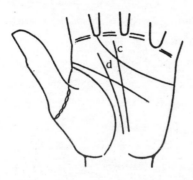

Fate line going to Saturn (c) and Jupiter (d)

If the line stops and then jumps to the thumb side of the hand, the subject will make improvements to his career and his financial standing at that time.

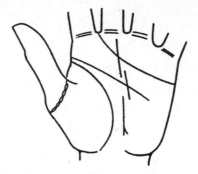

The fate line may shift from one side to the other

If it stops and then jumps to the percussion side, the subject will become more interested in his home and social life than career aspirations at the age of the jump.

When the fate line begins close to the wrist on the mount of Neptune, the subject is aware of his ambitions from an early age.

When a fate line starts at the middle of the hand (e), he will be self-motivated.

If the line starts at the lifeline (f), he will be self-motivated, but he will also receive a good deal of help and advice from his family.

If the line starts close to the percussion edge (g), outsiders will give him his opportunities in life and may be responsible for his motivation. He may also have to travel in order to fulfill his dreams.

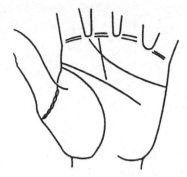

The late starter

When the fate line begins halfway up the hand, the person is a late starter. This may refer to a woman who can only start to put her mind to a career once her children are off her hands.

The illustration below shows interference on the line in the form of breaks and islands, and a line that stops short of its destination. All these interferences on the line refer to setbacks, ailments, financial problems, relationship problems or anything else

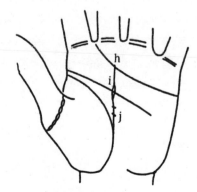

Setbacks and money worries

that puts the individual's life on hold for a while. A line that stops short shows that the person stops trying, possibly because things start to work out well for him.

If the fate line breaks up into a number of small lines traveling up the hand (k), the subject will have many tasks to cope with in life. This is often an indication of a period of self-employment.

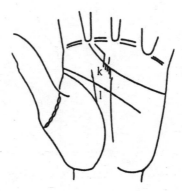

Self-employment and self-motivation

A secondary line that rises from the lifeline (l) shows a self-motivated fresh start, and this can often accompany the self-employment marks on the fate line.

A doubling of the fate line (m) shows that the subject is splitting his energies, possibly between the demands of home and work.

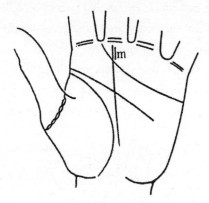

Doubling of the fate line

A long stretch of doubling shows dissatisfaction with life. If the doubling is, in effect, a long island, this shows a long period of emotional unhappiness or worry. I remember seeing a woman with a very long island on the fate line. She told me that she had spent years being angry and upset because her husband had left her for another woman, and her hand showed that she had put her own life on hold for years because of it.

Nails

7

Fingernails and toenails give a good indication of a person's current state of health and the state of someone's mind. Nails take about six to eight months to grow out, so they show what was happening at the time they were being formed, and to an extent, the body's progress while they grow. When assessing personality by the nails, one must take into consideration their size and shape and the size and shape of the fingertips beneath them.

Size

Large nails belong to a painstaking type of personality who prefers to live and work at his own pace; he doesn't care for changes and upheavals. He is capable of producing very detailed and carefully executed work.

Small nails denote that the individual lives at speed, he is competitive and he isn't great at dealing with details. He can be openly critical, while the person with the large nails can be just as judgmental, but he keeps his feelings to himself.

Shape

Those with nails that are square at the base find it hard to express themselves or to release energies from within their personalities. Nails and fingertips that are square belong to people who are good at figure work.

Very square nails denote practicality and capability, but a lack of imagination. The mind is attuned to structural ideas, such as mathematics, mechanics, farming, or building work or craftwork of all kinds.

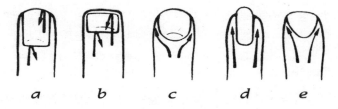

a   *b*   *c*   *d*   *e*

Long square nails (a) show a methodical nature. These people can be creative and quite deep in their thinking, but they lack vigor or speed. They may harp on about the past, but they are loyal and kind to those who need help.

Short square nails (b) denote an irritable personality that fears change, yet paradoxically also dislikes boredom. This person is quite hard to live with. He may be sexually aggressive, jealous and possessive, argumentative, critical or very cutting. Even in its mild form, people with this type of personality can be moody and difficult.

People with rounded fingernails (c) are sociable, emotional, creative and fairly harmonious, but they are easily bored and may lack power, vigor and strength of character.

Large round nails belong to a laid back person who likes to take his time over things. Such a person is rarely spiteful or difficult, but he lacks ambition, and he is probably idealistic rather than materialistic. He may not be a worldly success in the ordinary sense of the word, but he may be a great friend to the needy. This kind of person acts as a creative balance in this money-conscious world.

Small, rounded nails show restlessness and changeability. Sociable and creative, this type is more competitive and more critical than the other type, but he is sympathetic, helpful and friendly. His emotions may be hard for him to control, but his sense of humor will help him to keep a sense of proportion.

Narrow nails

A long, narrow nail (d) belongs to someone who would prefer life to be easy and free of too many responsibilities. This type of person seems to remain close to his parents throughout life.

Superficially charming, people with long, narrow nails may be selfish and babyish. They may be creative, but they are also materialistic and possessive. These subjects want the good things of life without having to spend too much effort in getting them. Extremely narrow nails show touchiness, long narrow ones show a mercenary nature.

Fan-shaped and spatulate nails

Small and fan-shaped nails (e) mean that the subject is an energetic, super achiever who has little tolerance of the foibles of others.

Ultra-small, fan-shaped nails seem to indicate a high level of self-indulgence, possibly in connection with alcohol, food, smoking or even drug taking. This person may be unreasonably jealous of others, or whiningly sorry for himself.

Truly spatulate nails are less fan-shaped and they have a panel of flesh showing on either side of the nail. These belong to active, inventive, slightly offbeat people.

When the spatulate nails are large and the finger ends splayed outward (like a spatula), the person is restless and inventive. He cannot sit still for long and may prefer a job that keeps him either on his feet or driving around the country. Although spontaneously kind, these people forget their friends as soon as they are out of sight. Their tense nature will make them competitive, either in sports or in business.

Pointed nails

People with pointed nails can be idealistic or artistic dreamers who never achieve much, but they are family loving, humorous, and kind-hearted.

Claw-like nails

When the nails resemble claws, the subject needs money and status. This type of person needs a comfortable life and he will make an effort to provide it for himself if there is no prospect of anyone else doing it for him.

Nails and Health

Fingernails and toenails describe events that happened to their owner during the previous six to eight months, and they can indicate even minor day-to-day changes by variations in their color.

Tiny nails

Problems with the stomach, bladder or kidneys. The subject is easily fatigued.

Watch glass or Hippocratic nails

When fingernails bulge upward in the middle and turn over at the ends, they are called "Hippocratic" nails or "watch-glass" nails and this used to be something that doctors saw quite often, as it was a classic sign of tuberculosis. It was also seen in the smoky towns of the industrial revolution, where people didn't get enough clean air to breath. It's also seen in cases of lung cancer, emphysema, heart disease or heavy smoking due to the damage to the lungs. The nails improve if the subject's health improves.

Clubbed finger-ends can also indicate ulcerative colitis or cirrhosis of the liver.

Circulatory problems will cause thickening and a characteristic yellowing of the nails, and there may be nutritional deficiencies, an under-active thyroid or even brain damage. However, I suggest that you take care not to jump to conclusions if you see nails like these, because they may simply be an inherited characteristic or even the result of damage from soaps and solvents.

White spots

White spots on the nails point to vitamin or mineral deficiency, such as a shortage of zinc, magnesium or calcium. These often show up in the late spring, after a dark cold winter when the lack of sunshine has caused a shortage of vitamins A and D. These spots can also be a sign of anxiety and depression.

Moons

If the moons at the base of the nails suddenly change, either by growing larger or by disappearing altogether, the subject may have heart problems. If the moons are normally small, non-existent, or very large that's fine, because it's only important when they suddenly change.

A blue or purple shade across or around the moons indicates heart trouble, possibly angina.

Tunnel nails

These nails are curved so that, if you look at them from the tip toward the wrist, they look like the roof of a tunnel or a Nissen hut. This shows a weakness of the spine, which most likely may have been damaged by the work that the person does.

Lateral ridges (Beau's lines)

These can indicate heart disease and Reynaud's syndrome, rheumatoid arthritis, or autoimmune diseases such as lupus. These lines can be caused by exposure to cold and by anorexia.

Longitudinal ridges

These denote problems with the bones, joints, cartilages, tendons, muscles and nerves surrounding the bones. If this appears on most of the fingers, the person probably has rheumatism.

If a ridge runs down one or two fingers, it's a sign of bone damage somewhere in the body. If the line appears on the thumb, the problem may be in the head, neck or spine. If on the index or middle finger, it could be on the middle part of the body. The ring finger suggests problems with arms and legs, and the little finger suggests problems in the hands or feet.

Lindsay's nails

If the tip of the nail is brown, the rest pink and the cuticle white, there may be chronic kidney failure.

Yellow nails

The nails are thickened, hard and yellow or greenish yellow; there may be respiratory or lymphatic disease, also thyroid problems (Grave's disease), or jaundice.

Splinter hemorrhage

Streaks due to bleeding beneath the nails are a real danger signal because this indicates high blood pressure or an infection in the lining or the heart, although it can also be the result of psoriasis.

Pitting

Irregular pitting is caused by psoriasis, while regular lines of pits are associated with alopecia.

Brown stains, freckles, and marks

If these appear on a white-skinned person's nails or cuticles, the subject could have a malignant melanoma (skin cancer).

Color

If nails suddenly change color from a nice, healthy pink, there is something wrong in the bloodstream. Any nail will lose its color when the end of the finger is pressed, but if the color is slow to return, the person is anemic.

Feet

8

My mother once told me a story about a cobbler who made and mended shoes in a half-basement in a small town in Russia. While he worked on his boots and shoes, he observed the feet and legs that he could see above him, passing by the window, and this set him thinking about the characteristics of people in conjunction with the way they wore out their footwear.

He concluded that exuberant, active and generous personalities wore out their soles beneath the balls of their feet, possibly due to a bouncy walk and a habit of spinning around on one foot. Those who wore out the edges of their shoes on the little toe side were mean-spirited and crabby folk who were frequently also tight-fisted. Those who wore down their heels seemed to be domineering and sometimes not quite in their right minds, while toe scrapers lacked confidence. I leave it to you to look at the undersides of your shoes and to contemplate the characteristics of their wear and tear . . .

Other snippets of folklore suggest that when a woman tucks her foot or leg under her body and sits on it, she is at ease with those she is with, such as family and friends.

Some men or women shake a leg or swing it back and forth rhythmically as a way of releasing unwanted nervous energy.

Bunions grow on those who do a lot for others and not enough for themselves.

A subject whose big toe is longer than his second toe is supposed to be logical, while one whose second toe is longer than his big toe is supposedly intuitive.

Reflexology

The theory of reflexology is that the body is divided up into zones, each of which corresponds to a particular area of the feet. When a reflexologist is asked to help with a particular health problem, he works on the part of the foot that corresponds to the relevant area of the body. Indeed, a skilled reflexologist can often tell what is wrong with his client by the condition of certain parts of the feet.

I remember some years ago, when I was traveling around, working at psychic and alternative health exhibitions up and down the country, spending a hilarious evening sitting up with about five or six friends on a bed in our digs, while Xian (pronounced Shan), a beautiful Chinese reflexologist, gave us an impromptu lecture. She demonstrated her art on our feet, which we lined up on the bed for her inspection. I remember that we all found her tweaking and prodding painful. Indeed, I shall never forget the sight of Malcolm Wright, the palmist, throwing himself across Berenice Watt, the psychic, and howling with a mixture of pain and hysterical laughter while Xian prodded and pulled his toes. Xian's theory was that the foot is like a miniature seated body, whose head is at the tip of the big toe, the bottom is at the heel and the legs and feet extend up the ankle.

I recently met another reflexologist called Gilly Sutherland, a woman just as beautiful as the lovely Xian. Gilly tells me that there are a variety of ideas and methods in use, but they all rely on the idea of zones, and most associate the head with the toes, and work back from there. The system that Gilly uses considers that the area related to the spinal cord runs from the edge of the big toe all the way down the inner side of each foot. The lower areas of the body are associated with the area around the back of the heel, and other soft organs are distributed around the sole of the foot.

In order to give you some idea of how it works without re-writing someone else's reflexology book, here is something that I've known for many years and that I've used to help others from time to time. When someone has a headache, massage the tips and the big pads of the person's toes fairly firmly, without twisting them or hurting them. If the headache is caused by tension, mas-sage the joints on the big toes and the edges of the feet adjoining the little toes.

One final point stressed by most reflexologists is that one should try to keep one's feet healthy and free from corns and calluses, as these cause a blockage or disturbance in the body's natural defense system.

While researching this section of my book, I came across yet another reflexologist named Hazel Goodwin; this woman has worked in the alternative therapy field for many years. Most people these days recognize that one cannot separate the mind, body and spirit, and that a malaise in one area will cross over and affect another. Hazel showed me how a reflexologist can pick up on emotional or spiritual problems while working on the physical ones. Hazel works the feet in order to clear any mental and physi-cal blockages and to restore harmony and well being to the whole person.

Lateral Zones of the Feet

The feet can be divided into five lateral zones as shown in the illustration below, each of which is associated with a particular area of the body and at the same time, a particular sphere of the patient's life.

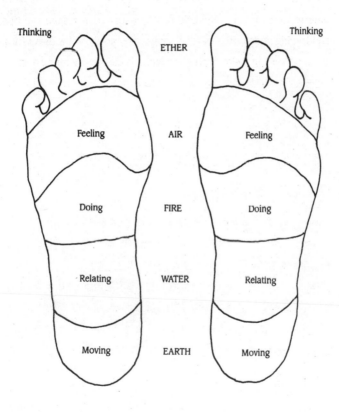

The divisions of the feet

The heel area

This is associated with the base chakra, the element of earth and the color red. On a physical level, it relates to the lower part of the body, the hips, thighs, legs and feet. On a mental and emotional level, this area refers to movement, so a problem here, either something wrong with the "feel" of the foot or something obvious such as hard skin, may reflect a physical disability preventing the patient from moving around, or a situation that is keeping him or her tied down. One example might be a young woman tied down by small children, while another could be of a person stuck in a job or a relationship that frustrates him. Other possibilities are of wanting to live elsewhere, or to travel more. On another level, the lack of movement can result from trying unsuccessfully to get some enterprise off the ground or trying to shake off lethargy.

The heel and instep area

This is associated with the sacral chakra, the element of water and the color orange. On a physical level it refers to the abdomen, while on a mental and emotional level, this area refers to relationships. All relationships can be difficult, and a problem here could indicate unhappiness in marriage, troubles between parents and children, problems at work, difficulties with neighbors or even the absence of a relationship.

The instep area

This is associated with the solar plexus chakra, the element of fire and the color yellow. On a physical level, it rules the middle areas of the body, which are the stomach, thoracic area, liver, pancreas and so on. On a mental level, this area refers to "doing," so a problem here would show that the patient is having difficulty with the practical side of life. While movement problems may cause temporary or permanent delays, something wrong with the "doing" area shows that the patient isn't doing what he should be doing.

The ball of the foot

This is associated with the heart chakra, the element of air and the color green. On a physical level, it refers to the heart, lungs and the areas surrounding them. On a mental level, this area refers to the function of feeling. This is a hard one to explain. A person can be too sensitive, both in the physical sense, by over-responding to heat, cold, pain and so on, or on a mental level by becoming upset too easily. Without the sensitivity of "feeling," we cannot understand the pain of others or notice what is going on around us.

The toes

This area is associated with the throat chakra, the element of ether and the color blue. On a physical level, it refers to the area from the top of the shoulders to the top of the head. On a mental level, this area concerns the function of thinking, so it doesn't need much explanation. A clear head and an active brain are always an asset, even when all the other functions are on the blink. To some extent, this area reaches upward even beyond the level of thinking, into the spiritual realms.

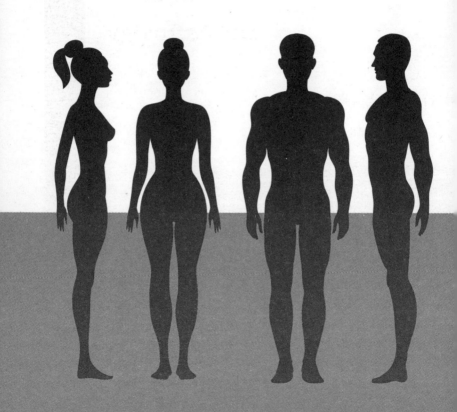

Influences of Color and Astrology

9

The conventions, myths, and taboos about color are amazing, and the reasons for this are positively Darwinian. Many animals have a strongly developed sense of smell, and bats have great hearing, but the ape family (of which we are a part) has evolved a strong sense of sight. Birds also rely largely upon sight, and if they could talk, we would probably discover that they also have strong views about color. In the animal world, color helps to identify foods that are poisonous or those that are ripe and ready for eating, but color also comes in useful for courting rituals. Some apes display brightly colored parts of the body in order to attract the opposite sex. For example, there is one kind of female monkey that has a pinkish heart-shaped area on the chest, which becomes red and prominent when she is ready to mate.

Have you ever considered why we dress baby girls in pink and baby boys in blue? The answer lies in the economics of color. In the past, pink vegetable-based dyes were cheap and easy to produce, while blue mineral-based dyes were expensive, so the exclusive blue color was saved for the more prestigious male child. Royal blue was so expensive to produce that it was reserved for those who carried blue blood in their veins. Mediaeval paintings of the Virgin Mary always show her dressed in a deep rich blue. As the wife of a Nazarene carpenter, about the last colors Mary could have worn were blue or purple, so she is shown this way as a mark of respect for her holiness. In Roman times, purple was so costly that it was reserved as a trimming for the tunics and robes of senators and other high dignitaries. Although lilac shades were possible by the early part of the 19th century, deep purple only came on stream toward the end of the 19th century, when chemical aniline dye manufacturing came into its own.

Interestingly, in many communities, in the days before the chemical and dye industries started, red or pink were the right colors for a baby boy! Pink is a mixture of red and white, and the color red is associated with the planet Mars, which has always been the planet and symbol of masculinity. Green was the color associated with Venus, so that would have been a suitable color for a girl.

A widowed Maharajah would not be allowed to wear bright shades of red, orange, green and so on. This would make sense, because the wedding saris on view in Asian shops are in very bright shades of red and green, with plenty of showy gold sequins and other decorations sewn on them. Western brides still like to wear a traditional white dress, even when the couple have been living together for years and have several children. In many eastern countries, white is the color of mourning. A British bridegroom is often hot and uncomfortable in his strange old-fashioned gray and black penguin outfit.

We have imported the yellow ribbon from the USA. Americans tied yellow ribbons around the trunks of trees in front of houses where women lived and waited for a lover or husband to come home from some war in one piece. Those who work in the New Age world love all shades of lilac, purple and mauve, as these represent the crown chakra, and by extension, psychism. In Italy, mauves, lilacs, purples are the colors of mourning.

Political colors are interesting. We all know what green politics are, but what about red ones? In Britain, the Labor party color has always been red and the Conservative Party's has been blue. The Liberal Democrats tend to favor yellow, but only came into being fairly recently. In the USA, the right wing Republican Party is always colored red on the election map, while the liberal

Democratic Party is colored blue. In 2004, elections in the Ukraine ousted an unpopular government symbolized by its blue and white flag, while a popular orange one was voted in. In Holland, orange represents the House of Orange, which is the Dutch Royal family. A distant connection of the reign of the Dutch William and Mary in Britain in the 1700s has left the Unionists with an orange flag as a legacy. The Catholics and southern Irish color is green, and their flag contains a large swathe of orange—but they call it gold.

Catholics and some other Christians use a color hierarchy for their priesthood. The priest wears black, the bishop wears purple, the cardinal wears red and the pope wears white.

Color, Astrology, and the Body

The signs of the zodiac and the planets are linked to various colors, shown in the following table.

In addition, each sign of the zodiac has a typical body type, as well as ailments that are typical of each sign.

Aries

There are two Arian types, with the lucky one being tall, thin and rather large-boned, while the less lucky one is short and rounded. Both types have a broad, somewhat rounded face and thin or difficult hair. Male Arians often lose their hair. The eyes may have a peculiarly flat look with puffy lids. The feet turn out when walking, but despite this, the Arian is a good walker and a good dancer. Aries is associated with sudden inflammatory ailments, eye problems and headaches.

SIGNS	PLANETS	COLORS
Aries:	Mars	Red
Taurus:	Venus	Green or pink
Gemini:	Mercury	Lemon yellow
Cancer:	The Moon	White or silver
Leo:	The Sun	Chrome yellow or orange
Virgo:	Mercury	Taupe, beige, light brown
Libra:	Venus	Green or pink
Scorpio:	Mars, Pluto	Dark red, magenta or black
Sagittarius:	Jupiter	Royal blue, purple
Capricorn:	Saturn	Grey, brown, black or dark green
Aquarius:	Saturn, Uranus	Electric blue or neon colors
Pisces:	Jupiter, Neptune	Sea blue green

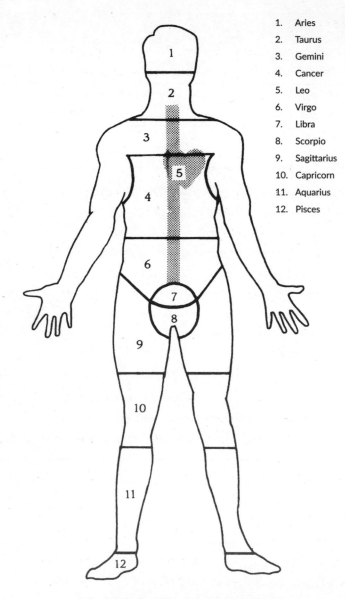

1. Aries
2. Taurus
3. Gemini
4. Cancer
5. Leo
6. Virgo
7. Libra
8. Scorpio
9. Sagittarius
10. Capricorn
11. Aquarius
12. Pisces

Parts of the body and astrological correspondences

Taurus

Typical Taurean people have a top-heavy body and a flat backside. Despite the heavy appearance, the subjects move gracefully. They often have lovely eyes and skin, good thick hair and a nice smile. The vulnerable areas are lower jaw and throat, including the thyroid gland and the neck.

Gemini

These people are short and slim while young, although they can put a lot of weight on in later life. They have bright eyes that look directly at whoever is speaking. Their hands and feet are small and bony with a slightly knobbly appearance. Vulnerable areas are the hands, arms, shoulders, upper respiratory tract and the nervous system. This sign also rules the mind. Many Geminis drink too much.

Cancer

These people have a rounded appearance with a chubby face and a nice smile, although some are thin with well-defined features. They move slowly and they are graceful. Their eyes are warm and their hands and feet are small. They have sloping shoulders and a deep rib cage. Some women of this sign have a large bust, but not all do. Vulnerable areas are the chest, lungs and breasts, also the stomach and upper digestive system.

Leo

A typical Leo has lots of hair, which is often worn long. Leos are of medium height and they become somewhat overweight later in life. Slow-moving and dignified, the stance and walk are regal.

Vulnerable areas are the spine, the heart, the arteries and the circulation.

Virgo

Could be any height and probably of medium weight, but with a slightly protruding stomach. They have very pale or very dark eyes that look directly at the person who is talking to them. They can put weight on in later life. Vulnerable areas are the lower digestive system and bowels, the skin, nervous system and the mind.

Libra

These people are of medium height and weight, with a pale complexion and light eyes. The eyes are often lovely and full of fun. They have a habit of holding one shoulder higher than the other. Their movements are quick and they walk quickly. Vulnerable areas are some of the soft organs such as the pancreas, bladder and kidneys. Also rules the ability to move and walk.

Scorpio

These people can be any size and shape, although they are often medium height and well built. They have well-defined features with challenging eyes that cannot be missed. Vulnerable areas are the sexual organs, lower stomach, lower spine and groin. They can suffer from blood disorders.

Sagittarius

These people are medium to tall, with long limbs, a long face and a nice smile. They have warm eyes that are never still. They may have large bones, but their movements are fast. Some have a lantern jaw. Vulnerable areas are the hips and thighs and the circulation through the legs.

Capricorn

These people range from small to medium in height. Their hair is neat, but rather fine textured. They have very good bone structure and nice eyes. Their movements are calm, slow and neat and they speak slowly. Vulnerable areas are the knees, skin, bones, ears and teeth.

Aquarius

Could be a little taller than the average and probably slim. Fair complexion, nice smile with a strong jaw line. These people walk, talk and eat slowly. They have a large and possibly twisted nose that gives the face an imperious look. Vulnerable areas are the ankles, the circulation to the extremities, and the breathing.

Pisces

The stature is short to medium and the person has a rounded, slightly protruding stomach. The complexion is pale, with a rounded face later in life. The hair can range from pale to dark brown, but it's often mousy. The eyes are arresting, being very pale or very dark and slightly protruding. The vulnerable areas are the feet, lungs and the mind. These people sometimes take to drink.

The Colors We Choose To Wear

There is also a theory that we can alter the way we project ourselves and even the way we feel by selecting a particular color to wear. I've asked people whether they give any thought to the colors they wear and for the most part, their answers don't relate to color symbolism at all. People dress for the weather, for what they happen to be doing at the time, for fashion, for what suits them and whatever happens to be lying about in their bedroom. Many women choose colors that enhance their eyes, hair or skin tones. Having said this, some men and women have strong feelings about colors and will only wear a small range of them.

The following explanation should help you to understand what it is you are absorbing into your aura or projecting out from it by habitually choosing a particular color.

White

White symbolizes innocence and freshness. This is symbolic of someone who is setting out on a journey in life, and starting something completely new. It's like a clean canvas waiting for an artist's inspired brush. We tend to associate white with doctors and dentists, and therefore, with cleanliness and professional competence.

Red

Red is the color of physical energy—the positive kind that allows one to get things done, or the negative kind that expresses force, anger and aggression. It's stressful, but also strong. Red is also associated with sexual energy.

Pink

This is a mixture of red and white, and it expresses femininity and the gentler side of sexuality associated with love, tenderness and feeling.

Orange

This is a mixture of red and yellow, and it's extremely forceful because it combines the physical energy of red and the mental force of yellow. This combination is great for achievement and learning, but can be a bit too strong, dynamic and dogmatic for some.

Yellow

Yellow is the color of mental energy and it's associated with intellectual pursuits. It's a helpful color to those who need to be able to think and concentrate, but it can be a bit too dogmatic or dictatorial for some. For some reason, yellow has become associated with cowardice, but it has also become linked to loyalty and to waiting for a loved one to return from service away from home.

Green

Green is a combination of yellow and blue, but it's also the color of nature. It's associated with growth and regeneration and is therefore a good color for those who work with living things or who wish to help or heal others. It's also worth wearing green if you are ill, as it will help the body to renew itself, and green is a good color in which to rest and relax. Green is popularly associated with jealousy. At one time, green was considered an unlucky color, and

I can remember people who wouldn't use green in their homes. Interestingly, there was something behind the evil reputation of the color, because green colored household paint used to contain arsenic. Many children lick or nibble paintwork, so before people made the link between the contents of the paint and the sickness and even death that green paint caused, they believed it to be unlucky.

Blue

Blue is the color of exploration and of mystery. The depths of the sea and the vastness of the sky are blue, therefore it's a good color to choose when you go on a mental or real journey. A purplish blue would be even more spiritual, while turquoise suggests personal growth resulting from the development of personal awareness. Popular songs describe feeling blue as being sad.

Purple, violet, lavender, lilac

These colors represent spiritual growth and the understanding of that which is hidden, so psychic ability or specialized knowledge is represented by these colors.

Black

Some see black as sophisticated, while others like to wear it for its slimming effect, but it can also be linked to unhappiness, mourning and fear.

Brown

This is associated with the earth and all its bounty, so it suggests the security of money. Brown is associated with nurturing, regeneration and creation of future prospects. Wear brown when you want to make some money!

Mixed colors

Mixed colors such as cream, tan, turquoise, aquamarine and so forth can be interpreted by reading each of the component colors. For example, cream is white with a dash of brown.

Body
Language

10

The term "Body Language" was coined by Julius Fast in the book that he wrote in the late 1960s. In the 1970s, the person with whom we most associated body language was the zoologist, Dr. Desmond Morris, whose books *The Naked Ape* and *Manwatching* are among his many best sellers. In this chapter, I'll take a brief look at body language and the way in which we use space.

Space and Territory

The Englishman's home is his castle—and so is everyone else's. We all need a space of our own for our home and we need a space to call our own at work. If that space is invaded, we become uncomfortable and we can even react in a hostile manner. The amount of space we need for living is relative to a variety of circumstances. The hard-pressed Japanese are used to living with very little personal space either in their tiny houses, at work or on their public transport systems, whereas the Australian sheep farmer considers that a neighbor who lives ten miles away is encroaching on his territory.

The space that we require around our bodies varies, too. In cities like London, we accept that we are going to spend some part of the day standing in a queue, jostling up against others in a busy shop or packed like sardines in a commuter train. We cope with this by avoiding the gaze of those around us, standing as straight and still as possible and losing ourselves temporarily in our own thoughts. Two people chatting in a crowd achieve the same thing by tuning out everyone around them.

Some years ago, I spent time in South Africa, and while I was there, several local people drove me around. Every one of my South African drivers reacted angrily when another car followed them for any length of time, and I noticed that in each case my driver became stiff and uncomfortable in his or her seat, and then exploded with angry remarks directed at the following driver. To my 'London-in-the-rush-hour' mind, these cars were following at quite a respectful distance, but to my wide-open-space friends it was an inexcusable intrusion.

Privacy and Safety

Human beings are very adept at sending out "leave me alone" signals in all kinds of public situations. I remember learning when I was a girl that if I sat in a cafe reading a book, I could become almost invisible, whereas if I allowed my eyes to roam around the room I was in danger of inviting unwelcome interest. However, this doesn't always work. I once had to wait for a colleague whom I had arranged to meet in a local pub, and after about 45 minutes, I realized he wasn't going to turn up. I looked up from my magazine and noticed someone watching me with too much interest. My intuition told me that it was time to leave; as I did so, I made sure that my movements were both casual and confident, gathering up my things in a businesslike manner and leaving smartly through the door to the car park. When I got back into my car, I locked the doors and left immediately.

What was it about the watcher that alarmed me? I can't put my finger on anything—there was just something in his body language that alerted me to potential danger. Our usual reaction to "space invaders" is to move away, thereby re-erecting the space barrier around us. Some aggressive people actually lash out when they feel invaded. Try fiddling with a totally non-aggressive woman's handbag and see what you get!

Dominance & Submission—the Status Game

Animals living in groups have a pecking order. The usual arrangement is that the strong, mature males are at the top of the list, with the weaker males, the females, the elderly and the young following on, in order of precedence. Human beings have many kinds of pecking order and many ways of reinforcing the authority of the dominant person or group. Ritualized respect may be shown by bowing, backing out of a room or, in some cultures, total body abasement. We consider it impolite to sit down in the presence of royalty or VIPs, and it would be a dreadful breach of etiquette to touch a member of the Royal family.

It is important to be aware of which country or society one happens to be when traveling, as there are many examples of the same body language having different, even opposite meanings. In the UK, men will tend to stand back and allow their superiors through a door, or out of a lift, first. In Southern Africa, tribal custom is the reverse—the men would leave first—the idea being to get out of your way! Similarly, when entering your office for an interview, the tendency would be to sit down immediately, without being asked. This simply indicates deference by not standing above you.

Sexual Attraction

When we spot someone that we fancy, how do we weigh up his or her potential availability? We unconsciously watch their body language. An attached couple will touch each other. The woman may perform a grooming action or advertise her ownership of her man by straightening his tie. He will cup her elbow as they walk into a room. Someone who isn't spoken for allows his or her eyes to roam around the room, and it will be easy to engage this person in conversation.

If a man notices a woman he fancies, he will give her a warm look with a hint of a smile. A woman will look at a guy and then turn away, but she will immediately begin to "groom" herself by touching her hair or brushing out imaginary creases in her dress. When a man tucks his thumbs into his waistband while at the same time allowing his fingers to point downward, he is giving an unconscious sexual signal. A woman who is sitting with her arms and legs crossed in a self protective manner and with her shoulders hunched is unlikely to be interested in a man's advances, while one who is sitting in a relaxed manner just may be.

If two people in a conversation begin to copy each other's movements, it's clear that they are interested in each other. Preening and grooming movements such as touching the hair are a kind of precursor to touching each other. As the evening wears on, the happy couple's heads come closer together. They breathe in each other's odors and begin tentatively to feel the textures of each other's clothing, maybe even their skin.

Loitering with Intent

While I was writing this section of this book, my friend Carol called me. Carol used to be a police officer, so if anyone should know something about body language, she should! Here is her description of a nervous loiterer who's up to no good:

"He's looking around, especially behind him, all the time. He walks up the road and perhaps back down it again in an uneven rhythm, with fast paces followed by slow ones. He doesn't know what to do with his hands or whether to keep them in his pockets or not. Oh, and he looks furtive and shifty somehow."

Such loitering behavior often expresses ill intent, or some impending threat. At the very least, it can be used to make someone feel uncomfortable and on the defensive.

When considering the intent of someone's behavior or body language, one point is worth considering: Different cultures behave in different ways. For instance, Britons tend to look at someone while listening and away when speaking, while West Indians do the reverse.

Handshakes

Shaking someone's hand has gone out of favor in our day-to-day encounters, although it still lives on in the business world. Business people tend to shake hands when they first become acquainted, while the French and other continentals shake hands with their friends of both sexes each time they meet. It's good to touch other people in this non-sexual and non-threatening way.

It used to be said that a businessperson could tell a lot about a person by the way he or she responded to a shake of the hand, and this seems to be born out by facts:

A strong, firm handshake belongs to someone who is comfortable within his own skin, and within the situation in which he or she is at the time. The hand is usually warm and pleasant to hold.

Someone who delivers a bone-breaking handshake either doesn't know his own strength or is a bully who is trying to impose his personality and desires on others.

A limp handshake, which makes you wonder if the person is actually alive, shows a lack of energy. The person might be ill, depressed or not a particularly strong personality. The hand is often rather cool and it might even feel a touch damp.

There is also the famous "election candidate" handshake, in which the political candidate shakes with his right hand and grips the person's arm with his left. This is supposed to convey real warmth and friendship and to make the other person feel special, or to convey gratitude to the person for supporting the candidate. I doubt whether a female candidate would give this kind of handshake, and I doubt whether a male candidate would give this kind of greeting to a woman. It seems to be an acceptable crossing of space boundaries between men, and that's it.

I recently read of a meeting between the then Senator Barack Obama and the then President George Bush. They chatted to some members of the public and shook many hands. When the session was over, President Bush took one of those little hand-sanitizers out of his pocket, squirted a little on his hands and then offered the bottle to Senator Obama, saying something like, "This will save you from picking up flu or other germs and taking them home to your family." Senator Obama took a squirt and then had to think about the implications, political and otherwise of meeting, greeting, and sanitizing!

Then there is the "secret handshake." This is well documented in freemasonry where members once needed to identify themselves to each other by secret means. Thus, if the person giving the secret handshake received the same handshake in return, he knew that he was in safe company. As far as I know, there are three handshakes. Two are in use by those who are training to become Masons and one by those who have taken "the third degree" and have become full Masons.

Gesture

In chapter 6, "Hands," I discussed gesture as a reflection of body part and what that indicates. However, hand gesture is movement, and so in this sense I will revisit the subject of gesture to see how it contributes to our body language.

Hands give a great deal away to a trained palmist. If you loosen your hands by shaking them a little and then hold them with the fingers pointing to the sky, the finger that curls downward will show what's on your mind.

- If the index finger is bent, your ego will be a bit deflated and you will be uncertain of your direction in life.

- If the middle finger is bent, you will be worrying about the practicalities of work, money and the security of your home.
- The ring finger may relate to hobbies and interests, but it shows stress in family matters when it's bent.
- If the little finger is curled, shows that you are not able to put your message across to others.
- If the little finger sticks up in a ladylike manner, your mood will be obstinate.
- When the little finger falls away from the other fingers, you need your privacy.
- A thumb that is curled into the palm shows considerable worry and possibly neurosis or fear.
- If the index finger pulls away from the others, you seek independence.
- A gap between the middle fingers suggests a state of rebelliousness.
- And finally, the late John Lindsay, a wonderful palmist, gave me this tip; to spot the dominant person in a relationship, see who has the largest thumb—relative, of course to the size and shape of the rest of the hand.

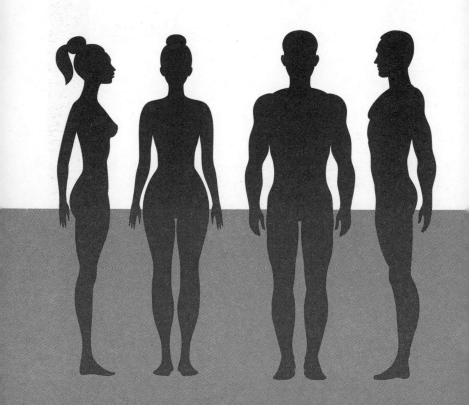

The
Little
Things

11

Sometimes the tiny things can say volumes about us! Body parts and body language are things that are obvious to us day to day—we are always, in fact, "reading" others by these larger physical indicators. But small things matter as well, and they are easy to overlook or not pay attention to. The two most common of these are moles and itches.

Moles

In days gone by, people considered that the position of a mole on the body suggested certain characteristics and a certain type of destiny for that person. When looking at moles, you should take note of its size, color, and shape because, while a collection of pale freckles won't mean anything, an isolated and obvious mole will. The larger the mole, the more important it is. If a mole is round, its effects will be beneficial; an oblong one is fairly lucky, but an angular one is considered bad. A dark mole has a stronger effect than a pale one, and a very hairy one is considered a very bad omen indeed, but a couple of hairs on a mole bring prosperity.

I hardly need to add that if a mole becomes itchy, crusty, changes shape, gets darker or begins to spread, you must ask your doctor to look at it.

Location of moles

1. A mole on the right side of the forehead shows that the person is going places in his career.
2. On the right eyebrow, the subject will marry when young and his or her partner will be very pleasant to live with.

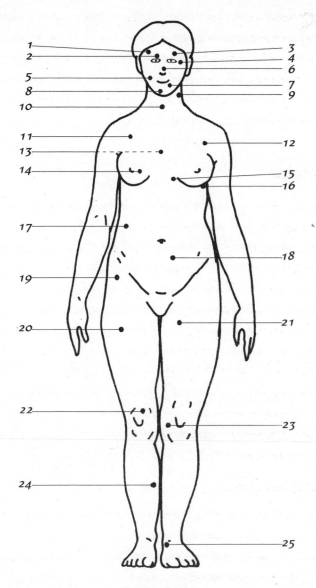

Location of moles

3. On the left of either the forehead or the eyebrow, unexpected disappointment.

4. A mole on the outside corner of either eye denotes that the subject is steady, sober and reliable, but may be liable to suffer a traumatic experience.

5. A mole on either cheek means that the subject will never be rich, but won't be particularly poor either.

6. A mole on the nose suggests success in all undertakings.

7. A mole on the lip suggests that the subject is stylish and fastidious. They are also lucky in love and they find it easy to study and to learn easily.

8. One on the chin shows luck and success with the career and business matters. This person will reach a position of status.

9. A mole on the neck means that the subject will narrowly avoid being suffocated! After this event, the subject will receive a large unexpected legacy and rise to a position of great status!

10. A mole on the throat brings wealth through marriage.

11. A mole on the right side of the chest or back denotes a fall in status and income. This mole also means that most of the individual's children will be girls.

12. On the left side of the chest or back brings success in business and a strong sex drive. Most of this subject's children will be boys.

13. A mole on any part of the back means that the person is a hard worker, with a responsible attitude to life.

14. A woman with a mole on the breast will have a mediocre life with no great losses or gains.

15. In a man, a mole on the left side of the chest over the heart denotes a kindly person who likes to ramble on. He is often slightly discontented, as he tends to chew things over too much in his mind.

16. In a woman, a mole under the left breast suggests that she will carry and give birth to children without difficulty.

17. A mole low down on the right side of the ribs suggests a slow thinker who is best left to do things at his own pace.

18. A mole on the belly belongs to a selfish, greedy, gluttonous and lazy person. This subject is also slovenly and dirty.

19. A mole on the hip indicates many children who will be patient, hardworking and a credit to the subject.

20. A mole on the right thigh brings riches plus a happy and lucky marriage.

21. A mole on the left thigh means poverty and a lack of friends. This person is also on the receiving end of hatred and injustice from others.

22. A mole on the right knee denotes an easy life and a good marriage.

23. A mole on the left knee belongs to someone who has a temper that can result in rash acts, but under normal circumstances, this person is cool, honest and decent.

24. A mole on either calf symbolizes a lazy, thoughtless person who lives for today and doesn't think ahead.

25. A mole on either ankle suggests that a male will be somewhat feminine or even effeminate in his manner, while a female will be courageous, active and a handful.

Itches

We are all familiar with the idea that when one of our ears is burning, someone is talking about us, or that when one of our palms itches, we are about to come into some money, but we may not be familiar with all the other itchy beliefs, so here is the full list:

1. If the crown of your head itches, promotion and an increase in salary are on the way.

2. If your right eyebrow itches, you will soon meet an old friend or you will be reunited with a previous lover.

3. If your left eyebrow itches, you will soon meet a friend who is ill, or you will see your old lover with someone else.

4. A ringing in your right ear means that you will soon hear some good news. An itch here means that someone is saying nice things about you.

5. A ringing in your left ear means that you will soon hear some unpleasant news. And, an itch here means that someone is saying nasty things about you.

6. A violent itching of the nose means trouble and worry is on the way (or an allergy like hay fever is about to act up).

7. Itchy lips suggest that someone is running you down behind your back.

8. An itch on the back of the neck means that someone close to you is about to suffer a violent trauma.

9. An itchy right shoulder means that you will soon receive a large legacy.

10. An itchy left shoulder means that you will soon be weighed down with troubles. It may also possibly be linked to some form of heart disease.

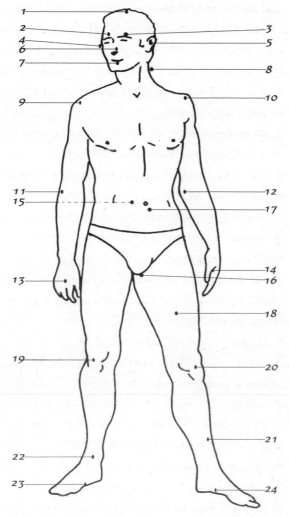

Location of itches

11. If your right elbow itches, good news is on the way.

12. If your left elbow itches, you will suffer a disappointment, or soon share your bed with a stranger or a strange person.

13. If your right palm is itchy, money is on the way to you.

14. If your left palm itches, you will have to pay someone else's debts.

15. An itchy spine means that heavy burdens are on the way.

16. An itch in the genital region means that you can shortly expect an addition to your family, or that you will soon be married.

17. If your tummy itches, you will soon be eating a sumptuous meal.

18. If either or both your thighs itch, you will soon be sleeping elsewhere.

19. If your right knee itches, your life will change for the better and you will also become interested in religion.

20. If your left knee itches, you will have a setback in life.

21. Itchy shins mean you may have a long, painful illness.

22. If your ankle joints itch, you will be united or reunited with a loved one. If you are already happily settled, your life will become even happier.

23. If the sole of your right foot itches, you will soon be on a pleasant journey.

24. If the sole of your left foot itches, you will soon be on a journey of a sad or unpleasant nature.

Legend has it that, if your left ear itches—meaning that someone is running you down—you should bite the fingers of both hands, and the person will soon get their comeuppance!